How To Cut Your Legal Bills in Half

Hugo N. Gerstl

How To Cut Your LEGAL BILLS in Half

A Guide to Reclaiming America's Promise: Affordable Justice for All

Millennium

An Imprint of The Millennium Publishing Group

Library of Congress Cataloging-in-Publication Data

How to cut your legal bills in half : a guide to reclaiming America's promise: affordable justice for all
Gerstl, Hugo N. (1941-)
CIP 99-067023
$21.95 hardbound
Includes Table of Contents, Index and Autobiography Page

    p.   cm.
    1. Self-help. 2. Lawyers. 3. Attorneys. 4. Legal System. 5. Mediation.
    6. Dispute Resolution. I. Title

ISBN 1-888820-07-1

Millennium
Published by Millennium Books
a division of The Millennium Publishing Group
P.O. Box 1994
Monterey, California 93942-1994

Distributed to the book trade by ANDREWS MCMEEL PUBLISHING

The author and publisher gratefully acknowledge permission to quote from

    Raptor, ©1992 by Gary Jennings, Published by Doubleday Publishing Company

    The Eiger Sanction, ©1972 by Trevanian, Published by Crown Books, Inc.

To Lorraine

Without whom nothing is possible,

and because of whom there are no limits.

And to the Memory of Gary Jennings,

the greatest writer of all.

Contents

*Legislation to limit the amount of the contingency fee; Abandonment of
"No Fault"—Defense now fights every case*

*Why proposed "solutions" won't work; Trial delay reduction Acts; Not
enough judges—and we can't afford more; Civil cases pushed "to the
back of the bus;" Outstanding judicial candidates can't afford to be
judges; "Fast track" benefits the wealthy; Lawyers cannot afford to
devote sufficient time to a single case; Discovery problems made worse
by "Fast Track;" Rent-A-Judge: Fast, smooth justice—if you can afford it;
Attractive to popular judges because of the atmosphere and money;
Denial of equal access to the law for those who can't afford it;
Arbitration: panacæa or cancer?*

*Opening lines of communication without lawyers; The mediation model;
Everyone wants to do what is in his or her own best interest; Everyone
has the right to define what their own best interests are; no one should
have the authority to decide for another; Giving away as little power as
possible; Setting realistic goals and expectations; What makes an effective mediator? How does mediation differ from arbitration? Arbitrator
makes a decision—Mediator assists parties in deciding on a resolution*

*Deciding you want to mediate rather than litigate; Selection of the
mediator; History starts now; Unlike trial or arbitration, which searches
for "the truth," mediation allows parties to move forward from "ground
zero;" Should an attorney or judge be a mediator? Paying the mediator's
fee? Mediation as problem-solving, not finger-pointing; Should lawyers
represent parties in mediation?*

Fifteen Practical Ways to Cut Your Legal Bills in Half

(Details start on page 167)

1. If there is a legal insurance policy available to you through a reputable company, look into it.

2. Get involved in organizations that provide free (or low cost) legal representation.

3. Write your senator, congressman or local legislator and find out what government-sponsored legal programs are available: Legal Services for Seniors, Rural Legal Assistance, etc.

4. Negotiate a firm, fixed fee or a "high-low" range for your legal representation.

5. When you are seeking a contingency fee lawyer, negotiate the percentage you will pay—never pay more than 25 to 33⅓ percent.

6. If the case is relatively simple, consider using a paralegal to help you with the paperwork.

7. Visit the County Law Library—and Learn How to Use It.

8. Try to get a mediation clause in any contract; if you can't get one, insist on an arbitration clause to resolve differences.

9. Talk—and keep talking—with your would-be adversary, his or her friend, or with anyone else who can get him or her to sit down and talk—before both of you decide to go to a lawyer.

10. Don't be afraid to question your lawyer's monthly bills.

11. Choose your lawyer as you would choose your friend.

12. Don't be afraid to change lawyers in midstream.

13. If you and your lawyer ultimately have a falling out over legal fees, demand fee arbitration.

14. If you must have a lawyer, insist on an understandable written contract.

15. Don't Telephone Your Lawyer Unless You Absolutely Have To!

Opening Statement

IT HAS BEEN THIRTY-THREE YEARS since I became a lawyer. While my respect for the rule of law has not diminished, there are inequities that must be addressed. It is so that you, the non-lawyer, can participate and understand, that this book has been written.

Litigation is expensive. Dealing with the legal profession can be exhausting, both financially and emotionally. But it need not be that way. There is a way to save or control the horrendous costs and cut your bills by a third, even by half or more. It is contained in these pages. In order to avoid the expense of litigation, you should consider embracing mediation as an alternative method of resolving disputes.

As a part of understanding why I have suggested an alternative to lawsuits, I have attempted to show why legal bills are so high and how they get to be so astronomical. I don't say this as a means of "lawyer-bashing," which would be a cheap shot at a profession that has treated me well, but rather to demonstrate that an intolerable situation has developed because we—all of us—have allowed it to happen. We have stopped communicating with one another and have allowed the resolution of our differences to spiral out of control—and the cost has escalated accordingly.

This book is not aimed at the criminal justice system, since the only experience most of us have in that respect is fighting a traffic ticket. Here, we will explore only civil litigation—resolving differences between one person and another or between a person and a company.

I've attempted to inject my theme of mediation as a cost-effective, emotion-effective alternative into many fields of human dispute. You, the reader, may find that some of these areas don't interest or affect you. For example, for many of us, the word divorce strikes a note of terror, and, like a bad dream, we don't want to read about it. Or if we are happily married (or, for that matter, happily single), it is simply irrelevant to our lives. Other subjects that I have written about in Chapters 10 through 13 may—or may not—be interesting. As with anything else, it all depends on where in your world you are standing at the moment you read this book.

While this entire subject cannot—and should not—be taken lightly, I have tried at times to sprinkle the seriousness of what I say with the sugar of laughter. This does not mean that I am trying to be flippant; it is just that law—like life—has its humorous moments.

Some litigation is unavoidable. But for the most part, if people approach a dispute with the attitude of, "How can this be resolved?" rather than "How can I destroy?" we will have made a wonderful beginning.

Law is Too Important
to Be Left to Lawyers

"This is a court of law, young man, not a court of justice."

**– Oliver Wendell Holmes, Jr.,
Former Chief Justice of the United States Supreme Court**

LAWYER JOKES have been around since ancient Greece. Although the most famous quote about lawyers, "The first thing we do, let's kill all the lawyers," comes from Shakespeare, Ben Franklin did pretty well when he said, "A countryman between two lawyers is like a fish between two cats," and Sir George Gay, speaking in the 18th century, could easily have been speaking today, when he said:

> *"I know you lawyers can with ease,*
> *twist words and meanings as you please;*
> *The language by your skill made pliant,*
> *will bend to favor every client;*
> *'Tis the fee directs the sense,*
> *to make out either side's pretense."*

However ironic, however bitter, however fearful these barbs may be, they have not managed to evade the naked truth: The American legal system has broken down and is failing to deliver justice. That failure is a drain not only on America's economy, but on the entire fabric of our lives. We have become a sue-happy society, using the courts as a lottery, a legalized means of financial or emotional murder, or a way to keep the pins of financial irresponsibility juggling in the air until, having wrung every possible delay out of an overburdened system, we conveniently file for the protection of the bankruptcy courts.

Not a pretty picture.

Ever since the late Middle Ages, when the developing European and English legal systems allowed lawyers to appear and argue a client's case instead of the principal having to do it for himself, lawyers have been convenient—and in many instances deserving—scapegoats for the ills of the societies in which they practice.

In every trial where an outrageous decision was handed down, people conveniently blamed "shysters" who prostituted the law to their clients' ends—or to their own. After all, it is always easier to blame another person than to accept responsibility for one's own acts.

We forget that in each of these trials lawyers did not make the decisions; juries made up of ordinary people like you and I— people possessed of *ordinary faculties,* who did their best to try to see that justice was done—made them. Or, if decisions were made by judges, the jurists were trying their best to follow laws enacted by elected legislators over a long period of time.

But finger-pointing doesn't cure the problem. All of us—judges, lawyers, legislators, homemakers, small businessmen, anyone who has had dealings with "the system"—particularly in civil law where our society tries to adjudicate differences between one individual and another—know the underlying problem: The legal system has failed because it fails to deliver justice in a timely, fair, economically efficient manner, and because once someone has experienced our system, they hesitate to go near it again.

I have been a part of that system for more than thirty-three years, during which I have participated in several thousand cases and have taken over a hundred cases to trial. Having been called everything from a shark to a junkyard dog, I only realized during the last ten years that our present adversarial system is no longer "fun." It is, plain and simple, a cancer, and none of us—lawyers, judges or laypersons—can live with it as it is much longer.

Make no mistake. I'm not a saint and I don't pretend to be. The practice of law has been good to me over the years. There have been many times when I've refused to take on new clients in order to allow me properly to serve the ones I had.

Those were times when ordinary people asked if they could see me, "only for a few minutes—I know you can't take me on as a client and I'll pay you for your time—I just want to ask your advice."

In my own life, people have said "No" to me enough times that I appreciate it when someone has a need simply to be heard. So I stole fifteen minutes here, half an hour there, and I listened to what these people had to say.

It dawned on me as I listened to them that more than ninety percent of these people did not need a lawyer—and that I would be stealing money from them if I took their case. There were people who had problems with their landlord over a $500 deposit. Or small tradesmen who had delinquent customers who owed them a few hundred dollars. Or adjacent landowners who argued over who should pay for their common driveway. These were "problems" that were capable of being resolved by a few minutes of cool thought and common sense, or, at the very worst, being resolved in Small Claims Court, where there are no lawyers and a case comes to trial in three weeks.

I can't remember one instance where I charged these people a cent for this "legal advice." Invariably I told them: "If I took money from you for what I just told you, you'd pay more than the whole case is worth."

But each time these folks left, I thought, "Someone else will charge them money. Someone else will see an opportunity to make money from this. Otherwise, why would these people have called a lawyer in the first place?"

The more I saw of these everyday people with problems that were serious to the point of threatening their emotions, but relatively small and simple for me, the more I became convinced that law as it is now practiced is a license to steal. Worse, because our society has become overpopulated with lawyers who somehow have to earn a living, we gouge it out of those who can least afford it—people who have children to put through college, men and women who struggle to pay the rent each month, older people desperately protective of what little they have left with which to live out their lives.

I became angry.

Not just at the legal profession, but at the way our society has been trained to accept what passes for justice in America.

And I became determined to write this book.

If I simply wrote a lawyer-bashing book, it would undoubtedly do very well commercially. Lawyers are people that everyone loves to hate. But if it did not provide constructive answers, it would line my pockets without providing any genuine service to others. It would be no less stealing than what I have accused many lawyers of doing right now.

It is time to change.

In order to do so, we must change our own perceptions of how the system should work, how we can best resolve differences among ourselves, and how we can control our own destinies.

And since lawyers are merely a reflection of our society, when we change the way we deliver justice, we will, at the same time, change the way lawyers operate.

CHAPTER 1

Why We Got Here

A businessman was about to visit a lawyer for the first time. He asked his partner, "Do you think I should wear my $2,000 suit, my fanciest silk shirt and tie and show up in my BMW so that the lawyer will be intimidated and influenced by my importance and power, or should I go down to the secondhand clothing store and buy an old sport coat and a frayed shirt, so the lawyer will be sympathetic toward me?"

The senior partner replied, "You know, the same sort of thing happened a few months ago when our secretary got married and she wanted to know what to wear on her wedding night. Her girlfriends advised her to wear a short, black baby doll nightie with a plunging neckline, wear a sexy perfume behind her ears and knees, and have soft, romantic music playing on the stereo. On the other hand, her mother advised her to buy a plain, white cotton nightgown with long sleeves and a high neckline, so she would come to bed as virginal as possible."

"I don't understand," the young businessman said. "What does this have to do with my problem?"

"It doesn't matter what you wear. Either way, you're gonna' get screwed."

URN ON THE TV any day or night of the week. You won't go an hour without being reminded of how central law is to our society—and how dramatic it seems to be. From the troubles in South Central Los Angeles to the multimillion dollar contract negotiated by the hottest sports superstar; from Kenneth Starr's spending over $50 million of our money to the seemingly interminable impeachment "trial;" and from O.J. Simpson's "Dream Team" to Paula Jones's $800,000 legal tab, lawyers are involved—whether they're being interviewed by Larry King Live, or shown in "courtroom drawings."

Minutes after the conclusion of the "Today" program, talk show hosts discuss perversions of the law that can only be termed bizarre. A wife, claiming years of abuse, cuts her husband's penis off. Each of them is tried for a separate crime and then they petition the court, through their lawyers, to let them spend Thanksgiving together. That's only the beginning. Scan the TV soap operas from ten in the morning to three in the afternoon. Lawyers as heroes; lawyers as villains; rich, powerful lawyers running society and politics. Messy divorces and messier murders, all glorified by trials, trials, and more trials. Wealthy scoundrels brought to their knees as juries award poor widows and orphans hundreds of thousands of dollars. Lawyers having affairs and lawyers catching others in affairs and filing huge suits for alienation of affection.

In between the programs, the sleazy advertisements for personal-injury lawyers who are "on your side" and who "fight for your rights."

No sooner do you come out of your interlude with the soaps than you are treated to Oprah or "Dateline," and more lawyer bashing, just before it's time for Judge Wapner (or the current "Judge," former New York Mayor Ed Koch) to preside over the "Peoples' Court" in endless reruns or to spend time with America's current sweetheart, Judge Judy.

The six o'clock news replays the day's gruesome and dramatic moments in the most current trial. Then it's "prime time," where you get a diet of "J.A.G.," "The Practice," the latest lawyer TV drama, or a recent movie, such as A Civil Action, which deals with law and lawyers.

In every instance, lawyers are portrayed as powerful, often sinister dealmakers—except for those young firebrands who scrape out a poor living proving that the system is wrong. We cheer when they beat the grand, well-oiled legal machine of the big firm, forgetting that tomorrow that "hero" will go back to living in a rundown rented apartment and shopping for the specials at Safeway, just like the rest of us.

If you think TV has glorified and vilified the lawyer, take a look at the latest bestseller list or the paperback novels near the checkout stand of any major supermarket. Of the top fifteen books on the best-seller list for fiction, it's an almost sure bet that at least five will be about lawyers, be law-related, or involve a courtroom drama. The books with the brightest covers (after romance novels, of course) are the lawyer dramas. John Grisham seems to have been on the best-seller lists forever.

In our fear of lawyers and the legal system, we have become exactly like observers who pass by a particularly gruesome automobile accident. We know it's not polite to look, or that we may become nauseated, but we take a quick look anyway—from morbid curiosity. And even though we know what we're going to see, we keep looking every time we pass another horrible accident.

Scott Turow and Steve Martini sell more books than Saul Bellow. John Grisham sells a helluva lot more books than Charles Frazier.

Books about lawyers generally sell better than books about owners of shirt laundries.

Why?

Because lawyers appear to lead more exciting lives than the rest of us. They seem wealthier, more powerful, larger than life. Lawyers seem to be on the black-and-white cutting edges of society while the rest of us lead lives of muted gray.

All this media hype has its effect not only on society, but on lawyers as well. The number of lawyers in the United States has quintupled since the early 1950s. We in the profession started to realize by the early 1970s that there was such a glut of attorneys that there could not possibly be enough work to go around.

A group of lawyers in the same locale has aptly been described as a "shark tank." Sharks do not suffer starvation or privation gladly. In the 1970s we saw a new, previously condemned practice become commonplace: the advertising lawyer. Although law has never been viewed by the general public as the noblest pursuit, its practitioners in the United States had, until then, considered it beneath their dignity to advertise for business like a common retailer, or worse yet, to advertise the prices they charged for their professional services. The dignity of the profession mandated that that simply was not done.

But there were too many young lawyers who, without advertising, could not compete with "establishment" firms. These young mavericks need to feed their families and their desires for luxury. They perceive that law, like anything else, is a business: you provide services, you get paid. And people will not find their way to your door unless you show them the way. By advertising.

For a while, bar associations tried everything possible to discourage advertising and to discredit or discipline the advertisers. Finally, the Supreme Court came down foursquare in favor of the consumer. The ordinary citizen had the right to know, and ethical canons which interfered with that knowledge were unconstitutional. The decision marked a great victory for the consumer. Or did it?

There is no such thing as "free." Neither the telephone companies nor the TV networks are known for their charitable beneficence. Nor are lawyers. Lawyers were finally free to advertise, but advertising was far from free. Someone had to pay the cost of the wonderful new means of letting the common man know that John Smith, the lawyer, was available. It wasn't going to be the telephone company and it sure as heck wasn't going to be John Smith. It doesn't take much sophistication to project who was ultimately going to pay the advertising bill.

Hourly fees started to escalate dramatically. Where once they had been $75 an hour—ten times what the average wage earner was making at that time—fees escalated to $200, $250, even $300 an hour. And the contingency fee for personal injury representation—that's where the lawyer doesn't earn his fee unless he recovers money for the client—went from 25 percent of the recovery to 40 percent or even 45 percent of the recovery.

The "establishment" firms that disdained advertising continued to charge the "prevailing" rate or recommended "minimum" fees suggested by their bar associations. And since the prevailing rate had risen dramatically, they felt it only fair that they meet or exceed that rate, for they felt they were by far "better lawyers" than the young dilettantes who advertised.

While the poor consumer was getting socked with lawyers' fees that were now beyond what any responsible, middle-class person could afford, three more bombshells were about to explode.

The first phenomenon—"creative billing"—had been known to the profession for years. One never spoke about it publicly, of course, but given a finite number of clients for whom to provide services, a finite number of hours in a day during which they could be serviced, and the lawyer's increasing office expenses and desire to live within (or beyond) the status he felt he deserved, it became necessary to generate additional billing.

An old joke tells of a lawyer who passed away and went to heaven. He was surprised to find that Saint Peter had arranged a grand reception and a marvelous parade for him. When the lawyer asked the reason for all the hoopla, Saint Peter explained, "It's because you're the oldest man that ever ascended to heaven."

"That's impossible," the lawyer replied. "I'm only forty years old."

"Not according to your billing records," replied Saint Pete. "They show you to be 137."

Lawyers bill creatively in several ways:

One of the oldest methods of creative billing is the "double team" method. Lawyer A, the senior partner, charges $300 an hour for his time. Lawyer B, his junior associate, charges $100 an hour. Lawyer A assigns Lawyer B to write a letter on behalf of the client. Lawyer B writes a draft. He presents it to Lawyer A for review and examination. After several such drafts, the letter is complete and the client is stunned when he receives an outlandish bill that shows both Lawyer A and Lawyer B, each charging their full rate, having billed for the letter *and* for an inordinate amount of time reviewing and redrafting it. If you, as a client, think you're spending a lot on a letter, think of the number by which you must multiply that when you engage in a lawsuit and must have a trial team representing you.

While this sounds outrageous, until very recently insurance companies and large corporate clients were paying just that, disguised somewhat by the fact that the large firms were giving "discounts" because the company was a "preferred client."

A second way of jacking up the bill is the "quarter-hour mini-mum" or the "point two" method of charging fees. In this practice, the lawyer, who keeps hourly records, does not keep exact minute-and-hour count, but rather bills in blocks of time. Usually the minimum a client will see on a detailed bill is measured in tenths of an hour or in quarter-hour increments. A telephone call that takes three minutes, for example, will be billed either as ".2 hour" or "¼ hour," depending on the firm's regular practice.

It doesn't take long to realize that even with a five minute phone call—and how many people do you think stay on the line longer than five minutes with a lawyer?—the lawyer could com-plete twelve phone calls in an hour. Twelve times five equals sixty minutes, right? Wrong. Two-tenths of an hour equals twelve min-utes. Twelve times twelve is 144 minutes, or more than two hours.

Suppose the lawyer's hourly charge is $200, a fairly standard rate nowadays. If the lawyer were charging by the exact minute and engaged in twelve five-minute phone calls, his bill would be $200 for that hour. But if the lawyer makes twelve phone calls for which he bills ".2 hour" each, the figure looks like this: $.2 \times 200 = \$40$ per phone call. And $12 \times 40 = \$480$ per hour. Pretty nifty. Even better if the lawyer bills in quarter-hour increments.

Nor is this practice limited to telephone calls. A letter that takes two or three minutes to dictate may likewise be billed at ".2 hour" or "¼ hour." And so forth. Welcome to the wonderful world of creative billing.

What's more, not only is this perfectly legal—many lawyers write into their retainer agreements that the client agrees that the minimum time that will be billed on any project at any time is .2 hour or ¼ hour. But lawyers have a smooth and plausible expla-nation for this financial sleight of hand: "Yes, Mr. Smith, I realize that your phone call only took five minutes, but you see, I was working on an important case at the time. By the time I inter-rupted my train of thought to respond to your very important call, thought about what you had said, made a mental note to check into everything you said, and got back to where I was before you called, twelve minutes—perhaps even more—had gone by." Try and prove that the lawyer's wrong.

A third form of creative billing is the add-on cost method. The client is invariably responsible for payment of the attorney's out-of-pocket costs. Usually that means the client is billed twenty-five cents for a photocopied page (ever think what would happen if Kinko's charged you twenty-five cents per page?); or five dollars for receipt of a fax transmission; or a surcharge for postage; or, in some cases, payment for the secretary's time.

The possibilities for perfectly legitimate "creative billing" are limited only by the parameters of a lawyer's own inventiveness, and no one has ever accused lawyers of being devoid of creativity.

The third "whammy" to be passed on to the consumer was that with all these wonderful new-old ideas, advertising, creative billing, and the like, there were still too many lawyers to serve the existing client base.

That meant lawyers had to create new kinds of lawsuits, and more of them, to insure full employment for their breed. In every community in which I have lived, I have found a great difference in the way doctors and lawyers think of and perceive their practice.

Doctors work cooperatively, but in inter-specialization. That means that while an ophthalmologist is delighted if another internist comes to town, since that means the internist may need to refer patients to him, he will fight to the death to keep another ophthalmologist from coming to town.

On the other hand, the lawyer's outlook is "If another lawyer comes to town, that means he will have to generate another lawsuit. For every lawsuit generated by that lawyer, there will have to be an opposing lawyer, and it may well be me. Welcome to town!"

From the 1970s forward, we have not only seen more new cases, but more new kinds of cases, with new causes of action for such things as "negligent infliction of mental and emotional distress," "breach of the implied covenant of good faith and fair dealing," and, of course, the extension of "civil rights violations" to just about anything from one's dog doing its duty on the neighbor's lawn to correctional officers failing to serve desired types of food to inmates.

I cannot—and do not—blame lawyers alone for this societal minefield. Clients—the public—were not unwilling sheep being led to the slaughter. I have had people ranging from the president of a large bank to one of the most successful merchants in the country tell me privately "We [bankers] [merchants], [etc.] are motivated by the same thing as you lawyers: greed."

The simple truth is that we Americans sue too much.

In all the world, only the Iranians come anywhere near the number of lawsuits and lawyers per capita as Americans. And they don't come close.

The number and percentage of lawyers in the United States is higher than anywhere else on earth; and in my home state of California, the number and percentage of lawyers is higher per capita than anywhere else except Washington, D.C.

We have gotten to the stage where five cents out of every dollar spent on **anything** in the United States goes to pay lawyers or their associates.

Even though the average lawyer's income increased 61% between 1983 and 1991, lawyers complain that they take home, on average, less than $100,000 a year; that many earn less than fifty thousand a year; and that less than ten percent of all lawyers in the country make enough to put them in the affluent category.

Regardless of the claim by insurance companies, credit card companies, banks and the like, that legal costs are too high and that there are far too many lawsuits, these "big boys" are the ones that profit most from the present state of the law. They can afford to hire mega-law firms—with the premiums that you and I pay— to carry on paper wars and eventually starve out the little guy. There is really no motivation for them to change the system as long as the premiums and the payments keep coming in. If you think my assessment is wrong, take a minute to think about who builds the fanciest buildings and who pays for developing the largest shopping centers. It isn't you and it isn't me.

Is the disease incurable?

The answer may be tied to another phenomenon that occurred in the 1970s. The Japanese invaded the American automobile market. General Motors and its brothers laughed derisively at the "rice burners," but when the dust had cleared, the American auto industry was in shambles. Only now is that industry coming back, and it is coming back only because it read the handwriting on the wall and reacted to American demand by producing better, more cost-efficient cars. The American public spoke with its pocketbook. It still has the power to do so.

If we want to change the law—and if we want to change the way lawyers operate—the solution lies within all of us.

CHAPTER 2

How We Got Here

"When the state is most corrupt, the laws are most multiplied."

— Tacitus

HILE ANCIENT ECHOES of Roman Church law still sound softly in America (the most apparent example being annulment of a marriage instead of divorce), the most direct link to American law comes from her parent country, England.

Legalese "words of art" filter down today, for no other reason than that they have been used "forever." In Saxon England, the basic administrative district—equivalent to the modern county—was called the *shire*. The chief law enforcement officer was the shire rief. In late 20th century America, the shire rief has become the County *sheriff*, who serves *writs* (written words of command sealed by the court), much the same as did his forebears a thousand years ago.

As London developed, so did commerce. That commerce quickly spread to surrounding towns and villages with the growth of numerous commercial trade fairs. It soon became necessary to govern trade at the fairs, whether by a system of (hopefully) honest weights and measures, or by enforcing contracts. As time when on, the markets became more sophisticated. The law of trade, called the "Law Merchant," came into being. Its laws became today's Commercial Codes.

The basic law from which we derive our current practice is the English "common law," a body of law that grew from day-to-day dealings among the citizens of England. As society became more complex, formal laws were issued by the king or, after the Magna Carta in 1215 AD, by the king and parliament. The interpretation and often the execution of the laws was left to the courts—called to this day the King's Bench (or, if there is a female monarch, the Queen's Bench).

Well, good and simple, right? Wrong.

For in addition to the law, the King's chancellor assumed a special jurisdiction that overrode the written or the common law—the jurisdiction "to do the right thing." That was called "equity"—impartial "fairness,"or the application of principles of fair dealing to supplement statutory law.

The concept of what constituted fairness was not locked in concrete. Chancellors were only human beings, with the same prejudices as other human beings. They lived and they died. What was fair to one chancellor might not necessarily be viewed as fair by his successor. A common 16th century jibe was that "Equity is as long as the chancellor's arm." Different chancellor, different arm's length. Does it seem outlandish that if the law itself was meant to be fair, there was need for a "fairer" legal practice? Of course.

Yet, in late 20th century America, there continues to be two distinct types of civil law: "Law" and "Equity." Although we Americans think we are a nation of laws and not of men, who are guaranteed a right to trial by jury, that is simply not the case. Every jurisdiction in this country has two divisions: legal practice and equitable practice. Some states have different courts for equity and law. Some states try legal cases and equitable cases in the same court. But in all states the rule is the same: You are entitled to a jury trial in *legal* cases, but **not** in *equitable* cases. Equitable cases include such things as:

1) Obtaining an injunction to stop someone from doing something
2) Divorce
3) Compelling someone to perform a contract—such as transferring title to real property
4) Reforming an ambiguous contract to make it truly reflect the intent of the parties
5) Rescinding (voiding) a contract that is inherently unfair

Although there were "large" firms in the 18th and 19th centuries, with as many as forty lawyers, the practice of law was exem-
plified primarily by the solo general practitioner, just as medicine
was dominated by the good country doctor. When you came to
the lawyer's office, which was often cluttered, with a roll-top desk
and a musty feel about it, it was to execute the sale or purchase of
a home, to prepare a will, to draft a lease or a business agreement.
Lawyers' letterheads of bygone days proclaimed the dignity of
times gone by. We did not go to "attorneys." We went to Counselors at Law. We went to receive counseling in our legal rights.

Indeed, when we spoke of lawyers, we referred to them as
"counselor," and in very polite, if somewhat archaic, conversation,
some of us still do.

Slowly, the term "Attorney and Counselor at Law" replaced
"Counselor at Law." By the middle of the 20th century, we had
dropped all pretense. Anyone who still used the term "counselor"
was an old fuddy-duddy, a throwback to the days of the horse and
buggy. Now it was "Attorney at Law."

Somewhere along the line, lawyers stopped being counselors
first and advocates second. They became advocates first and counselors only as a last resort.

Did lawyers lead the change or were they merely reacting to a
society that had become ever more confused, sophisticated, frustrated and litigious? It's the old "Which came first, the chicken or
the egg?" question, and there is no simple answer.

Whatever the answer, as society became meaner, it did not by
any means become leaner. In 1940, tens of thousands of civil law
cases were filed in the United States. Ten years later, the number
was in the high five figures, still relatively controllable. But by
the mid-1980s well over 200,000 civil lawsuits were filed in the
United States. The courts had lost the ability to control the incred-
ible proliferation of litigation.

More judges were appointed, more clerks were hired, and more
support staff filled ever-larger courthouses, until the money was
exhausted. The flow of frustrated, tenacious litigants and their
lawyers, seeking justice at the hands of the overcrowded courts

began to see waits of two, then three, then five years before civil cases could be brought to trial.

In California, the law provided that all civil cases must be brought to trial within five years, or they would be dismissed. By 1982, the Los Angeles County Superior Court was regularly starting cases on the last day of the five-year period. No sooner had the first witness been sworn in than the trial would be continued for an additional two years or more. The courts had fulfilled the statute to the letter, but litigants knew they might well be dead before their cases were adjudicated.

As society became still meaner and violent crimes escalated dramatically, a number of states passed laws that discouraged plea bargaining (where, in a criminal case, a defendant will forgo a trial and plead guilty to a lesser offense in exchange for a lighter sentence than he or she might otherwise have gotten). That opened the door of criminal pretrial proceedings to public scrutiny. The result was that many more district attorneys and criminal suspects chose to take their cases all the way to trial, leaving ever smaller judicial resources to deal with the civil law calendar, which, even before the changes, had been the stepchild of the law.

What followed—the "fast track" system and the resulting techno-litigator—has been a cure worse than the disease. In theory it is wonderful. The typical statute reads that "all cases will be managed so that they are finally tried within two years."

In fact, "fast track" has made the legal system less affordable than ever for the middle class. It has stacked the deck in favor of the wealthy. It has created law firms with well over 200 lawyers, assigned case litigation teams, "techno-litigators," and still more pressures on already over-extended judges and clerks.

The end result has been that if you are wealthy and can survive the expense, you will surely achieve substantially more than justice—provided your attorneys' fees and costs are paid. Of course, the vast majority of us simply can't afford the system.

Techno-litigation

"The law often allows what honor forbids."

– Saurin

 S LATE AS THE 1940s, when a client walked into a lawyer's office, he normally entered a somewhat Spartan waiting room where there might be a receptionist who doubled as the lawyer's secretary.

Enter today's techno-office and you'll find that it occupies several stories in the classiest area of town. The waiting rooms, the conference rooms, and the senior partners' offices are not only designed by the most expensive interior decorators money can buy, but their walls are adorned with museum-quality art. Usually when you enter, there is a single receptionist, who doesn't waste time answering telephones. Every call that comes in is computer-directed to a specific lawyer's "Voice Mail." You may leave a message of any length, though you'll probably be billed ".2 hour" for your trouble.

There is an electronic hum as automatons disguised as human secretaries pull up form after premanufactured form in their network-connected computer terminals. All one need do is take form number 4,194, change the names from "Smith, Plaintiff vs. Jones, Defendant" to "Baker, Plaintiff vs. Chanticleer, Defendant," and voila—$2,000 more in billing.

In addition to the immediately visible costs of running the technologically superior law factory—machinery, equipment, postage, telephone systems, computer retrieval systems, law library, and the like—are the "big ticket" items so often overlooked: malpractice insurance, which can run as much as $10,000 per lawyer per year, health and disability insurance for everyone in the office, paid vacations, law firm retreats, and a plethora of luxurious underpinnings. Small wonder that every lawyer in every major office in the United States is told that he or she must bill a minimum of 2,200 hours per year to remain in the good graces of the senior partners.

When members of the law firm are required to travel, even within an hour of their office, the client is billed for mileage, food, travel time, parking, and per diem allowance. Air travel has generally been first class or business class. Lawyers do not normally expect to stay at Motel 6®.

Clients are required to pay for all out-of-pocket costs associated with the lawyers' representation, from depositions to experts. All of these, incidentally, are legitimate expenses and will be discussed at length in a later chapter.

When it comes to billing, lawyers are akin to the Swiss mountain guides described so delightfully in Trevanian's *The Eiger Sanction*.

"There was a half-hearted attempt to organize a rescue team, but more in response to the desire to do something than to any hope of reaching them alive. In manifestation of typical Swiss compassion, the Bernese Oberland guides haggled over wages until it was too late to bother with the rescue....

"These men of the Bernese Oberland are fine mountaineers, always willing to face the rigors and risks of rescuing a climber trapped on the face of a mountain. But they never fail to send a carefully itemized bill to the man they have saved or, that failing, to his next of kin....

"Back at the hotel the next day, he received his bill. It seemed that, despite the double fee, there were many little items still to be paid for. Among these were medical supplies they had not used, food for the bivouac (Jonathan had brought his own to test the freeze-dried rations), and a charge for '¼ pair of boots.' This last was too much. He called the guide to his room and questioned him. The guide assumed an attitude of cooperation and weary patience as he explained the obvious. 'Shoes wear out; you would not deny that. Surely one cannot climb a mountain barefooted.

Agreed? For Matterhorn I usually charge half a pair of shoes. Eiger is more than half the altitude of Matterhorn, and yet I only charged you for a quarter pair. I did this because you were a pleasant companion.'

"'I'm surprised you didn't charge me for wear on the rope.'

"The guide's eyebrows lofted. 'Oh?' He took up the bill and scanned it minutely. 'You are perfectly right, sir. There has been an omission.' He drew a pencil from his pocket, licked the point, and painstakingly wrote in the neglected item, then corrected and checked the total. 'Can I be of further service?' he asked."

A lawyer's billing is handled so creatively by "the computers," that it is virtually impossible to successfully challenge the accuracy of the system. Every base is covered, and the client pays for every cent of it.

In my own office, a two-lawyer office with three clerical employees, which qualified as a small firm by any standard, we maintained six modem-equipped computers tied to a network, two laser printers, a laser fax machine, six telephone lines, including an 800 number, and a high-speed photocopier. Although we managed to cut our costs by sharing a conference room, our modest library cost us nearly $1,000 a month to maintain and our six telephone lines exceeded that sum by a substantial amount. All of that to keep up with the technology that has invaded every city, town, and hamlet in the United States. The average monthly cost for us to keep our doors open, before my partner or I took one dime of draw, was $30,000. That's a lot of billing for two lawyers.

Happily for the consumer, there's an interesting trend going on among the supergiants. They're starting to collapse under their own weight.

When economic times turned tough in 1990, major corporations and insurance companies started to do something they had never thought of doing before: they started using in-house counsel (salaried employees) almost exclusively, and, worse yet for the major law firms, they hired independent lawyers whose only job was to scrupulously examine the volumes of bills the company received from outside law firms and match them to commercially reasonable expectations.

To top that horrible (to the large firms) development, corporate clients started demanding that work be done on a fixed fee, per-case basis.

Although no one has ever accused large corporations and insurance companies of being the consumer's best friends, their sudden concentration on the profligate monies they were paying law firms marked a significant turning point. Now, lawyers, like every other business professional, would have to become competitive in pricing and cost-effective in service. Country-club-based senior partners, who would never dream of lowering their dignity to discuss the disgustingly "unprofessional" issue of fees, suddenly found that they not only had to talk about them. They had to face an angry marketplace and do something about them.

The result has been dramatic. Giant Finley-Kumble, a nation-wide firm known as the most aggressive and detested (even by the profession) shark tank in the country, collapsed and filed for bankruptcy. And the then-largest law firm in the world, Baker & McKenzie, totally eliminated its Los Angeles office and downsized by twenty percent. Other large firms, finding themselves with defecting clients, seriously declining revenues, high-priced contract talent, and long-term, expensive leases, started back-pedaling furiously, simply to stay alive.

Smaller firms, with smaller overhead and the ability to react decisively and with flexibility, have reacted to the downward economic spiral by adjusting the ways they do business, and have rushed in to fill the gap, offering services to corporate giants. But even the smaller firms can only cut overhead by a certain percentage without sacrificing quality of representation and the ability to generate the mountains of paperwork still required by court fights.

In the end, lawyers and the public are still very much married to each other, whether or not they want to be. The crisis we've managed to put off for years—perhaps centuries—is now very much upon us.

The public can no longer afford to pay the price of the technology that fuels modern litigation, but lawyers cannot afford **not** to utilize that technology, if litigation continues to grow at the rate it has in the past fifty years.

Unless all of us—lawyers and clients alike—face the fact that the irresistible force is about to meet the immovable object, and readjust our conception of how the law should—how the law **must**—work for everyone, we face nothing less than the total breakdown of the legal system as we know it.

CHAPTER 4

The Contingency Fee—
What Price Justice?

After the conclusion of the case, the lawyer shook hands with his client, who had gotten a wonderful settlement. The next day, the client received the bill. The client, reeling in shock, called his lawyer and said, "This says I have to pay $1,000 now and $500 a month for the next five years. It sounds like I'm buying a Lexus." The lawyer responded, "You are."

ACK IN THE 1950s the late Melvin Belli, self-styled "king of torts," and several other personal injury lawyers justified a new trend in the law called the "contingency fee." A contingency fee is one where the lawyer becomes the client's partner in the profits, with one exception: the lawyer is not liable for the costs. In the event a contingency lawyer advances any costs, the client owes these costs as a debt. The out-of-pocket costs are the client's responsibility, regardless of whether the case is won, lost or settled.

The contingency fee works as follows: the lawyer agrees to take the case with no set fee for the hours put into the case. If the lawyer wins or settles the case for the client, the lawyer receives a percentage of the settlement. In most states, the percentage of recovery is not limited or set by law, so the lawyer and the client can come to any agreement they want. Until the mid-1960s, a fee of a quarter to a third of the gross recovery was fairly common. From the late 1960s forward, the percentage that went to the lawyer has risen. Today, the most common fee arrangement provides that the lawyer will receive a third of the gross recovery if the case settles before trial, 40 percent of the recovery if the case goes to trial, and 50 percent of any punitive damages that may be recovered.

In theory, that benefits the client who could not otherwise afford a lawyer. The injured person who would be at the mercy of the insurance companies now has an advocate to even the playing field. In practice, there have been tremendous abuses of the system on both sides. There is no doubt that having a lawyer dramatically raises the dollar amount of the settlement or verdict. But it is a drain on the insurance industry, the plaintiff (the injured party), and our society.

In saying this, I know I am alienating the plaintiff's bar, but the sad truth is that the contingency system, which was originally designed to help the impecunious plaintiff, has gone too far. The plaintiff's unrealistic expectation of manifestly unreasonable settlements, the occasional million-dollar verdict, and the downright fraud that has been practiced on both sides in personal injury litigation, have created a game where the plaintiff's lawyers and the insurance companies are the winners, and the public at large is the loser.

One caveat about contingency fees: In virtually any case except an automobile accident, a serious personal injury case, or a "slam-dunk" wrongful termination case, your chances of finding a lawyer who will take your case on a contingency basis are slim to none.

There are three types of lawyers who take cases on contingency. The first is the general practitioner, who looks to "P.I." (personal injury) cases as the "fat" that supplements his hourly fees. Although these generalists like to believe they do a great deal of work in the area, their efforts amount to a negligible percentage of today's personal injury contingency fee work.

By far, the vast majority of business goes to the "PI mills"— what most "working" members of the bar generally refer to as "the sleazebags of the industry." These "mills" are run by sharp businessmen who just happen to have passed the bar, usually on the third or fourth try.

Most lawyers despise the "mill" lawyers for two reasons:

1) They give lawyers an even worse name than they already have. And, much more relevant,
2) They have, by sheer business acumen and outright chutzpah, soaked up more than 90 percent of personal injury business, which has always been the easiest and most lucrative part of law practice.

Ralph (that's not his real name) is typical of the breed. He graduated from a night law school while he was working in a department store. A lawyer is not allowed to practice law anywhere until he has passed the bar examination, a rigorous three-day test of book-learning knowledge. Ralph flunked the bar exam the first four times out. Finally, on the fifth time, he squeaked through. Most trial lawyers enjoy the rough-and-tumble of a jury trial. Ralph tried a case once. He was soundly and embarrassingly trounced. From then on, he vowed he would never try a case again.

Ralph came to our town twenty years ago. He saw the area as fertile for his projected personal injury "mill." As he once remarked to me, "The tree was loaded with nice, fat plums about to drop, and no one was there to pick them."

Ralph's operation was slick and smooth from the very beginning, and he set to work with a vengeance. He started by doing the unthinkable: he advertised heavily on local TV. He bought full-page, garish ads in the Yellow Pages. He listed a number of offices and telephone numbers throughout the area. His ads contained bold statements such as, "The insurance companies have people working to deprive you of your rights. We know dozens of ways to defeat the insurance companies at their own game." "You need a tough fighter on *your* side." "YOU DON'T OWE US A DIME UNTIL WE COLLECT FOR YOU!!!"

Like most "mills," Ralph's firm did not operate under his own name. Rather, he used a series of firm names that were both folksy and impressive: the "Accidental Injury Recovery Legal Clinic of North America—Helping the Injured is our *Only* Purpose," or "National Personal Injury Justice Project."

Ralph's ad appeared in more than thirty yellow page directories throughout the state, each with a local number to impress the readers that Ralph was a local fellow who operated right in their neighborhood. In truth, all of the numbers rang in to Ralph's real office (singular), thanks to a hundred "call-forwarding" lines. Every few years, when Ralph's unpaid yellow page advertising bill would get up over $200,000 and the telephone companies would threaten to sue him, Ralph would hire the largest firms not only to defend against those suits, but to countersue the phone companies for "mistakes" in his ads, or for "fraud" in not giving him the very first ad under "Attorneys" in the Yellow Pages. Apparently his ploy worked: his is always the first and largest Yellow Page ad you see in every directory in which he appears.

Ralph is not looking for a sophisticated client base. If a reasonably intelligent client somehow gets caught up in Ralph's advertising net, that's a happy accident for Ralph. As a general rule, he caters to the poor and ignorant of our society. The vast majority of his clients are from the low or low-middle income strata.

Ralph's cars and offices contain the most powerful, high-tech equipment, constantly tuned to police band radios to hear reports of any serious accidents. Never mind chasing ambulances; Ralph is usually at the scene ahead of the ambulance. Although it's been illegal for years, he employs "cappers"—nurses, aides, janitors, in the hospital, who quietly pass his cards around or strongly recommend him as "the best Personal Injury lawyer I ever knew." In extreme cases, they offer to telephone Ralph. "He can be up here and start helping you out in a few minutes, 'cause unlike most lawyers, he doesn't mind working nights and weekends."

Ralph puts on a wonderful show. He is as handsome as any movie star, with wavy hair and stunning clothes. He has a particularly nice touch with his clients on their first visit. Many of his clients can't afford the gasoline to drive to his office. Ralph maintains a large white limousine with a personalized license plate. He arranges to have a uniformed chauffeur drive the limousine to even the poorest area of town and makes an ostentatious show of picking up and returning the client home after their visit to Ralph's exquisite, tastefully designed offices. Very, very impressive.

Ralph has devoted his practice to one thing: making money. Lots of money. And he has been eminently successful. He owns palatial homes in several upscale resort areas. He is currently building a villa in Spain. His children attend the finest private school in the area and he regularly makes substantial contributions to the plaintiff trial lawyers' association.

Once, not too long ago, Ralph was quoted as telling a group of young people that the only way to know if a lawyer is good is to find out whether he is wealthy. "There is no such thing as a good lawyer who is not very wealthy, and if the lawyer is not wealthy, then he certainly can't be any good. Public defenders and deputy district attorneys work where they do only because they aren't good enough to find a job anywhere else."

The state and local bars have tried on several occasions to investigate Ralph's practice, but he has always stayed "just this side of the line." Although he is typical of the breed, he is by no means alone in his practices. He normally takes 45 percent of the recovery, where a general practitioner would take a third. He justifies that by saying he advances all costs for the client, and from start to finish the client never lays out a penny of his own for medical treatment or anything else. He rationalizes that since he is taking all the risk, he should be entitled to more than the "average" contingency lawyer.

As soon as the client retains him, Ralph makes certain that the poor, injured party is sent to an "appropriate" health-care provider—usually a very compliant chiropractor, neurologist, or orthopedic surgeon who knows the game only too well, and who has made hundreds of thousands of dollars through Ralph's referrals. The doctor knows exactly what Ralph wants to see on the medical report, and Ralph pays very well, about $250, to get such a report. The doctor also knows that this particular patient's treatment will be significantly extended, both in time and in price, and that the doctor and the physical therapist whom he employs will be well compensated.

The practice of sending a personal injury patient to a doctor who shares the lawyer's opinion that this patient has undoubtedly suffered more than any other patient who ever had soft-tissue injury, is not limited to the Ralphs of plaintiff's personal injury practice. Any attorney who does even a modicum of personal injury work for any period of time has a favorite doctor or group of doctors to whom he sends his client-patients. The defense bar has their own set of doctors, too. Only these doctors, whom the defense interests call "independent medical examiners," somehow don't believe that people are ever seriously hurt, or, if they are, they can usually recover in four to six weeks, provided they are left alone.

Many of these healers on *both* sides would threaten lawyers with libel and slander suits if they knew what they were being called behind their backs by the lawyers: "plaintiff's whore" or "defense whore" are the most usual appellations. The physicians invariably have impressive credentials, have testified on occasion for both plaintiff and defendant (although never in the same case), and, although some of them are candid enough to admit what they truly are, most would be shocked to think that they had sold out. But that is precisely what they have done.

The Ralphs, who give personal-injury law a bad name, and the general practitioners who dabble in personal-injury law, represent two types of contingency lawyers. The third type is the true heavy hitter, the plaintiff's major personal-injury specialist. The heavy hitter does not bother to advertise except in a dignified way that emphasizes the very substantial nature of his practice. He is well known to general practitioners, who will refer cases to him when they don't have the financial capacity or specialization to handle the case. His name frequently appears in state and national bar journals, the national media in connection with mammoth verdicts, or in respectful hushed whispers at bar conventions. The late Melvin Belli was the best known of the breed. There are others in large and small cities all over the United States.

The heavy hitter's firm knows that the client cannot afford to front the phenomenal costs of fighting a well-heeled automotive manufacturer, aircraft manufacturer, or physician's insurance carrier. The question of the client advancing costs is rarely, if ever, raised. The heavy hitter simply assumes that he will have to advance as much as a million dollars in costs for the client before there is even a semblance of an offer on the table. With such high stakes at risk, the heavy hitter knows he must get a superb settlement or result from a trial, since without that success, he will never be able (and does not expect) to get any of the costs back from the client.

The heavy hitter usually operates out of a large firm with a splendid support staff. He retains nationally known luminaries as his experts in virtually every field, and he pays them very well to share his view of the case. He is the lawyer who gets the multimillion-dollar verdict that you read about in the paper or hear about on TV. This type of lawyer is not interested in whiplash cases, the $10,000 to $20,000 settlements that feed the Ralphs and the general practitioners. He is looking for the quadriplegic, the brain-damaged, the passenger who was thrown out of a poorly built truck and fried in the gasoline explosion that followed.

Such lawyers are outstanding, well-organized trial machines, the pride of their profession in every sense of the word. For your sake, I pray that you never need such a lawyer, not because he or she will drain you financially—which he or she generally won't—but because if he takes your case, you will generally be so seriously injured that you will never have the quality of life that will allow you to enjoy your financial gains.

Occasionally, a lawyer will take a "flyer" by taking a business litigation case on a contingency. These are few, far between, and relatively high-risk, high-percentage (the lawyer usually takes 40 to 50 percent) cases. But, as a practical matter, don't expect a lawyer to take your "surefire winner" case on a contingency basis. He or she has been around the block often enough to evaluate the case for what it's worth—primarily to himself or herself.

The "Ralphs" of the legal world have recently had to face two startling new developments that may just put them out of business, or, at the very least, change the way they do business:

1) The insurance companies have combined with consumer advocate groups (strange bedfellows indeed!) to try to get legislators or voters to pass laws that limit the percentage contingency lawyers can charge, with increasing levels of success; and

2) After realizing that their never-ending, trial-lawyer-bashing quest for "No Fault"—a system that would essentially deprive the injured party of a jury trial based on the other party's negligence and simply compensate victims according to a formula, was simply not going to be approved by the legislators or the voters, the insurance companies got smart. They set a value on any given case (usually by using a formula) and then "drew a line in the sand." If a case did not settle at or below their offer, they would take every single case all the way through to trial, regardless of the expense, knowing that the "Ralphs" of the legal world, who depended for their living on **never** trying a case, would slink away or settle the case cheap.

The insurance companies, like big business, led the way—by sheer weight of their overwhelming economic power—to their own revolution. Concurrently, they, too, exercised their financial muscle to produce their own version of managed care: they would pay the defense law firm "x" dollars per hour or per case, **period.** Take it or leave it. And for those who left it, there were a hundred hungry firms that lusted after the steady paycheck each month.

Does this mark an improvement? Or will it lead to a further breakdown of the legal system? To use a legalism that has become an all-too-truism, "The jury is still out" on that question.

CHAPTER 5

The Stuff of Nightmares: The Anatomy of a Case from Start to Finish

"To seek the redress of grievances by going to law
is like the sheep running for shelter to a bramble bush."

– Dilwyn

TEPHEN KING NOVELS are scary but fun. Lawsuits are scary, but they're never fun. The experience an average litigant goes through in a lawsuit makes what happens to Stephen King characters seem merciful, which is one reason I, for one, try to avoid watching any drama on TV that has anything to do with lawyers or the law, and why I will read a law-related novel only if there's not a good book on statistics or the Middle Ages lying on my night stand.

Let's take a relatively simple dispute and follow it through a typical trail from origin to resolution in the present court system.

Art Owner and his wife Mary own a 1,500-square-foot home in a middle-class area of town. They decide to add 1,000 square feet to the house, consisting of two bedrooms, a bathroom and a family room. They don't need to put it out to bid because their friend, Bob Builder says he'll take care of the job on a "cost plus" basis. Builder gives Owner a "Standard Contract" that he bought at a stationery store, and where it provides for price, he writes in "cost plus basis."

Owner is a little concerned because he wants to know exactly what it is going to cost. Builder tells Owner not to worry about it, but if it will make him feel happier, it'll cost Owner about sixty dollars a square foot.

They shake hands. Owner goes to his bank and secures a loan of $70,000 to be on the safe side. Builder comes out with a crew the next day and starts measuring, pounding stakes, and tying string from one stake to another. Mary is delighted that things are moving right along, because she's heard so many horror stories about contractors and add-ons. She was a little nervous about the whole thing to begin with, because finances are rather tight.

Within three days, a number of subcontractors come to the job: plumbers, electricians, stonemasons, sheet-rock installers, painters, carpet layers, and roofers. The Owner home is a beehive of activity: everyone seems to be measuring, writing, figuring. Builder tells Art and Mary Owner, "See, I told you we'd get right on it."

Mary asks how long it will take. Builder assures her it will take sixty days, ninety at the most. Mary is concerned because the rainy season will start in about sixty days. Builder smilingly reassures the Owners that there will be no problem at all.

For the first month, things go wonderfully well. There are two or three men on the job every day. Although they seem to leave earlier each day, the skeleton of the home addition is becoming more noticeable all the time. When Builder presents his bill at the end of the month, Owner says it seems a little on the expensive side.

Builder tells Owner not to worry; things are always more expensive at the beginning—that's when he purchases all the materials and supplies, and when most of the work gets done. After telling Owner that things will lighten up real soon, he drops the word that he has to pay the subcontractors fifty percent up front—as a good faith progress payment—and that he'll need that money within a week because the subcontractors want to start work immediately.

Owner writes checks to the subcontractors the following week and Builder, at Owner's insistence, gives him receipts.

There is no work at the house for the next five days. Owner calls Builder. Builder's response is hardly comforting.

Builder stammers that he has run into a little problem with the electrician. He had two other jobs. He thought he'd be finished with them last week, but things went a little slower than planned. He promises Builder he'll be there first thing Monday morning. Builder sadly mentions to Owner that the project can't go any further until the rough wiring is in.

"What about the other subcontractors?" Owner asks.

"Well, the truth of the matter is, they're all kind of stacked up, sort of like planes waiting to get into an airport. The electrician has to do his job first, then the plumber, and so on." But Builder tells Owner not to worry, he's done hundreds of these jobs before. He'll get this one done on time and within Owner's budget.

Monday comes. The electrician doesn't. The project is quiet. Four more days go by. No one appears. Owner telephones Builder. Builder is not there, but the receptionist assures Owner that his telephone call will be returned as soon as Builder, who is out bidding another job, returns to the office. Owner's call is not returned.

After a very nervous weekend, during which Mary blames her husband for not putting the contract out to bid in a businesslike fashion, Owner is furious. On Monday, he telephones Builder's office again. There is no reply. No one comes to the house. That evening, Owner telephones Builder at home. Builder is noticeably cool.

Owner tells Builder in no uncertain terms that Builder had promised that the electrician would be on the project more than a week ago, and Owner has not even heard from him.

Builder responds that Owner must have his dates wrong; that the electrician was supposed to come in the *next* two days.

Owner claims he is certain that Builder told him the electrician was supposed to be there *last* week, but now, in an attempt to regain control of his temper and the situation, Owner asks for the electrician's number so he can call him direct.

Builder says that won't be necessary. He's the general contractor. He's responsible. He'll call the electrician and get him to Owner's house first thing tomorrow morning.

A week goes by. No electrician and Builder is "not available" when Owner calls. The following Monday, Owner storms into Builder's office.

Builder shrugs helplessly and says he didn't know that the electrician had a drinking problem. He vows to get another electrician on the job right away.

"But I've paid half the amount of his contract, already!" Owner explodes.

Builder reassures owner that he'll get the money back from the electrician, but meanwhile he will need another $5,000 to get the new electrician. He promises Owner this will be worked out at the end of the job. He'll make sure Owner gets a credit.

At the end of seven months, the addition is still not completed. Mary has started seeing a psychologist because of depression brought on by the situation. The plumber has filed bankruptcy without completing his job and the suppliers who provided the fixtures are threatening to sue Owner because they've never been paid.

So far, Owner has paid $84,000—$24,000 more than Builder orally promised him it would cost. When Owner returns home from work one day, he finds an envelope from Builder addressed to him. It is a detailed bill for an additional $25,000, including change orders, extras, and administrative charges.

The next morning, Owner calls John Barrister, a lawyer recommended to him by his brother-in-law, and makes an appointment for that very afternoon.

Barrister listens to Art and Mary Owner with a sympathetic ear and nods his head sagely. He scribbles notes on a legal-sized yellow pad, looks at a couple of thick law books, and says to the Owners that he can see why they're very angry about this situation, and they certainly have a right to be. However, he cautions them, there may be some difficulty because not everything is in writing, and the Owners and Builder may have different understandings about what the contract means. Barrister tells them he thinks he may be able to help them. The case may not be easy and it may take time, but he's optimistic he'll get them a good result in the end.

"It seems awfully simple to me," Mary says. "Builder didn't do what he was supposed to do, when he was supposed to do it. We didn't get what we paid for."

Barrister says he certainly understands her point, but, he claims, Builder will probably fight the case and bring all the sub-contractors in. He then advises them that he charges $200 per hour and that he'll need a $10,000 retainer.

"Ten thousand dollars?" Art asks, wide-eyed. "The whole project was only supposed to cost $60,000. Will I at least be able to recover my lawyer's fees?"

Barrister glances down at the contract, then looks up ruefully. He tells them that, unfortunately, there's nothing about attorney's fees in the contract. That means that under the American system of law, they cannot recover lawyer's fees from the other side. But the good news is that if the Owners lose the case, Builder can't recover attorneys' fees against them, either.

The Owners are aghast. How can they possibly lose the case? It's black and white.

"Not so black and white, really," Barrister explains. "There are a lot of holes in this contract. For example, there's nowhere in the contract where it sets a $60,000 cap, nor is there a provision that says exactly when the addition will be done."

Mary, about to break down in tears, gulps that Builder *promised* them...

But, the sympathetic Barrister explains, that promise is not in writing. Many laws require that the terms of a contract be reduced to writing and that oral promises may not be enforced. Indeed, he tells them, the very words of the written agreement say, "This contract is the *entire* agreement between the parties." That means that although he'll try to get the oral evidence about Builder's promises in, the judge may keep it out because of the "Statute of Frauds."

"I'll say there's fraud!" Art shouts. "The man didn't do what he was supposed to do, and that's certainly fraud!"

Unfortunately, Barrister continues, that's not the way the law defines fraud. But he assures them that he will certainly do the best he can to help the Owners and that he will aggressively pursue their case to the best of his abilities and make sure that a judge or jury fully understands their case.

When Owners ask Barrister how many other cases he is working on at the present time, he tells them "about eighty," but assures them not to worry, that his associate will work on this case and he'll be supervising her every step of the way.

As they leave the lawyer's office, a downcast Mary suggests to her husband that perhaps it would be best just to take their lumps, pay Builder off and ask him to finish the job. She worries that perhaps they'll end up even deeper in debt than they are now.

Driven by his pride, Owner vows he'll never let that crook Builder get away with this, and, if necessary, he'll go to the highest court in the land to see that justice is done.

True to his word, Barrister sends a letter to Builder outlining the Owners' case and demanding redress. It is not long before Barrister receives a letter back from Defensor, Builder's lawyer. Defensor points out that the Owners themselves are in breach of their agreement to pay Builder and that Builder would be very happy to finish the job in a timely manner provided Owners pay his very reasonable bill. He also writes that Mary Owner made several changes, asking for plugs on different walls than originally contemplated, and more expensive toilet and shower fixtures. Defensor suggests that Barrister ought to be making a claim against the subcontractors who, after all, are the ones who may have botched the job.

Negotiations break down. Barrister regretfully advises the Owners that they have only two options: give in the Builder's outrageous demands or file a lawsuit. The Owners reluctantly authorize Barrister to file suit. Barrister then files the first suit paper. In most courts this is called a "Complaint" or a "Claim for Damages." The Complaint contains a number of "Causes of Action"—legal theories of recovery.

To a non-lawyer, it would be simple to write a straightforward *precis* of what happened and ask the court to make a ruling that is fair and just. Unfortunately, over the years the law has developed various legal and equitable theories that must fit into pigeonholes set up by the law.

There are essentially three "large-scale" theories of recovery into which lawyers fit various causes of action:

1) **Contract actions**—causes of action which center around the performance or non-performance of a contract.

2) **Tort actions.** A tort is any non-contractual wrong. If you are hit by a car, you are the victim of a tort. If someone libels or defrauds you, you are the victim of a tort.

3) **Actions in equity.** (Remember that in an earlier chapter we talked about these special "no jury" actions to accomplish fairness and equity).

Barrister fires off a complaint loaded with many causes of action. He makes sure all three types of action—legal and equitable—are covered. When the Owners read it, they are impressed with its thirty pages. According to the complaint, the Owners seek damages for:

1) **Contract actions:** Breach of written contract; breach of oral contract; breach of implied-in-fact contract; money had and received.

2) **Tort actions:** Fraud and deceit; negligence; intentional infliction of mental and emotional distress.

3) **Actions in equity:** Rescission of the contract; reformation of the contract (to make it say what the parties really intended but forgot to put in writing); unjust enrichment; and specific performance (to compel Builder to complete the contract in accordance with what the Owners believed the contract to say).

The Owners ask the court to award them general damages for pain and suffering, compensatory damages for all of their out-of-pocket costs, exemplary and punitive damages because of the "fraudulent and oppressive" wrongdoing by Builder, all of their costs of suit (but not their attorney's fees), and "such other and further relief as this court shall deem just and equitable."

When he reads the complaint, Owner gleefully tells his wife that this will certainly teach that crook a lesson. They feel comforted that things are moving right along when they see the "Summons" that is going to be served with the complaint, because it orders Builder to file a written response within thirty days or he will face a default judgment.

Thirty days go by. On the thirty-first day, Art Owner calls Barrister and asks if Builder has responded to the complaint.

No, Barrister tells them. Builder's lawyer, Defensor asked for a thirty day continuance to answer the complaint because he's in trial. Of course Barrister gave the postponement to Defensor since that's ordinary professional courtesy and he would expect the same from Defensor.

After another thirty days, Owner calls again. Barrister tells him that Defensor asked for another continuance because he is taking his annual vacation, "but I promise you there will be a response within the next three weeks."

True to his word, the response arrives three weeks later, but it is not an "Answer." It is a pleading called a "Demurrer" (or, in Federal courts where they have abolished the Demurrer, a "Motion to Dismiss." (Elapsed time: 51 days). A Demurrer (lawyers pronounce it "de-merr") has nothing to do with the merits of the case. It is a legal document that challenges the complaint on the basis of **form.**

In this case, Builder's lawyer files a Demurrer on the basis that the electrician, plumber, stonemason, roofer, carpet layer, and painter, all of whom were "indispensable" parties, have not been sued. Builder's lawyer has entered an "Appearance" for Builder by a classical delay tactic. Builder's lawyer schedules the Demurrer for a hearing thirty days from the date he files it. (Elapsed time: 81 days).

Now Barrister has to file a "Response" to the Demurrer. But Barrister has additional court matters pending and no time to attend to the Demurrer, so he asks Defensor for a two week postponement of the hearing. Defensor, of course, returns the professional courtesy.

On the morning the Demurrer is to be heard, 95 days from the date the Complaint was filed, the Judge has thirty-five other short matters to hear. He decides that there are serious questions of law and form, that he hasn't had ample time to study the Complaint, the Demurrer and the Response because he has been hearing an average of thirty short matters (called "Law and Motion") for each of the last several days. Accordingly, he takes the matter "under submission," and promises the two lawyers he will rule on the matter "shortly."

Fifteen days later (Elapsed time: 110 days), the Judge sustains (grants) Defensor's Demurrer and gives Barrister thirty days to file an **Amended** Complaint to cure the defects of form. Barrister files his amended complaint within the time provided (Elapsed time: 140 days).

Defensor responds thirty days later (170 days elapsed) by filing a second Demurrer, which is heard four weeks later (Elapsed time: 198 days). This time, the court only takes ten days to overrule the Demurrer (Elapsed time: 208 days), and gives Defensor thirty days to file Builder's "Answer."

Defensor files Builder's Answer thirty days later (Elapsed time: 238 days); concurrently he files a "Cross-Complaint" against the Owners for breach of contract. At the same time, he files a Cross-complaint against each of the subcontractors for indemnity. It takes him thirty days to locate and serve legal papers on all of the subcontractors. (Elapsed time: 268 days).

Immediately the Plumber, who had, in the interim, filed bankruptcy, files a Demurrer to the Cross-Complaint on the grounds that the only Court where a case against him can properly be tried is in the Bankruptcy Court. By the time the dust cleared and the Court issued a decision, another 45 days had gone by (Elapsed time: 313 days).

Thirty days later (Elapsed time 343 days), the Owners and the other Cross-defendants file their Answers to Builder's Cross-complaint. But at the same time, each of the subcontractors sues one another and Builder and Owner in "Cross-cross-complaints" for indemnity and contribution according to the percentage of fault imposed upon each of them.

By the time everyone had finally asked for and received "professional courtesy" continuances and answered everyone else's Cross-complaints and Cross-cross-complaints, 410 days—one year and forty-five days—have elapsed. The case is not even in a position to be set for trial.

About that time, Barrister ruefully presents the Owners with a bill showing that $5,000 of the $10,000 retainer fee has been exhausted.

The legal skirmishing over the "pleadings" (formal lawsuit papers) has now come to an end, but the worst is about to begin.

In days of yore, law had an element of blind-man's bluff to it. Those old enough to remember the old "Perry Mason" TV series will recall that invariably, at the last possible moment, just after the last commercial, the hero came forth with a surprise that knocked everyone's socks off—a hitherto undiscovered witness, piece of evidence, etc.

Starting in the second third of the 20th century, courts and legislatures decreed that we should do away with the "sporting theory of litigation" by opening up the floodgates of Discovery. That means that each party is afforded an unprecedented series of weapons with which to force the opposing side to disgorge not only everything material to his case, but any evidence that is either relevant to the subject matter of the case or reasonably calculated to lead to the discovery of admissible evidence.

And if one party has made out a *prima facie* case that indicates the opposing party might become liable for punitive damages, that party has the right (subject to certain privacy protections) to obtain everything about his opponent's financial condition.

Today the arsenal of discovery possessed by each side usually includes, at a minimum:

1) The unrestricted right to take **Depositions** of all parties, their agents, employees, representatives, associates, partners, and anyone who was or could have been a witness to anything relevant

to the subject matter of the lawsuit or reasonably calculated to lead to the discovery of admissible evidence.

A Deposition is a court-sanctioned invitation that a party or witness cannot refuse to attend. It usually takes place in the opposing lawyer's office suite or in a conference room provided by the deposition reporter. The party or witness is questioned under oath by all opposing lawyers. Usually that party's own lawyer does not ask any questions of his client because he presumably knows everything his client is going to say and doesn't want the client to give any more information than necessary.

The party or witness may be ordered to bring certain papers, records, documents, or other things to the Deposition and may be questioned with respect to those items.

Even though a Deposition usually takes place in the informal atmosphere of the lawyer's office, it has the same solemnity as if it were in a court of law. The witness or party is placed under oath by a certified shorthand reporter, who records all proceedings on a stenotype machine. Nowadays a large number of depositions are videotaped as well.

A Deposition may be used to impeach the testimony of the party or witness, to support that testimony, or, if the party or witness is unavailable, to substitute for it. Most seasoned trial lawyers almost literally try their case at the deposition stage. There is no set time in which a Deposition must be completed. The longest deposition I ever attended involved five lawyers representing five sides and consumed an aggregate of twelve days spread over a one-year period.

Although the party's or the witness's lawyer has the absolute right to object to a question and instruct his client not to answer on any one of a number of grounds, the opposing lawyer will often go to court at a later time to obtain an order that the party or witness—the deponent—answer these objected-to questions.

Depositions may be taken in a cooperative, orderly manner, or they may turn into a battle of egos where one lawyer goes on a "fishing expedition" and the other "stonewalls" to prohibit virtually any discovery.

At times like these, the court may impose sanctions against whichever party or his attorney is at fault for the breakdown in the orderly Deposition procedure. The court may add an additional requirement: that the Deposition will be retaken before a referee appointed by the Court at the parties' expense. The referee is empowered to act in place of the judge, and he or she may impose monetary sanctions on the spot if there is an abuse or misuse of the discovery process.

The costs of the court reporter and the videographer are borne by the party who takes the Deposition. If the Owners' lawyer, Barrister, takes the deposition of the Builder, Painter, Electrician, Stonemason, etc., the Owners advance the costs of the deposition—usually about $500 to $800 per day—plus their own attorney's fees for that day.

At the end of the Deposition, the court reporter transcribes the Deposition proceedings into booklet form. The original of this booklet is presented to the witness for his or her examination and signature under oath. At the time he or she reviews the Deposition, the witness may make corrections. Any lawyer for any party can comment on these changes when the case goes to trial, particularly if there is a material deviation between what the witness said under oath and what the booklet reflected after the corrections are made.

Each attorney usually orders a copy of each Deposition, at a cost of about $300 per day's transcript. The transcript of the twelve-day deposition I described was $3,500 for each 12-volume set, and it was a cost borne by my client.

In theory, the costs of the deposition are recoverable if the Owners' lawyer obtains a favorable verdict. But more than 99 percent of all filed cases eventually settle before the court or jury makes a decision, with "each side to pay his or her own attorneys' fees and costs." So the hapless Owners will more likely than not be saddled with thousands of dollars of additional costs.

2) **Interrogatories.** These are written questions that require responses under oath. California has recently limited the number and complexity of Interrogatories, but most states place no limits on them other than the standard, "relevant to the subject matter

of the lawsuit or reasonably calculated to lead to the discovery of admissible evidence," and even California has liberal provisions for avoiding the statutory limitations.

I have seen Interrogatories run to hundreds of pages of questions.

Usually the lawyer, not the client, frames the Answers to these Interrogatories in such a way as to give as little information as possible and to avoid being "nailed down" to a position.

As with Depositions, if one side feels that the other has cheated by not properly and completely Answering Interrogatories, the lawyer for that side goes into Court and requests an Order compelling further Answers to the them and also requesting monetary sanctions against the recalcitrant party.

3) A third discovery tool is the **"Request for Admissions of Fact and Genuineness of Documents"** ("Request for Admissions").

In the first stage of a lawsuit—the pleading stage—virtually none of the pleadings—the formal lawsuit papers—are under oath. Thus anyone can accuse anyone else of virtually anything, with total impunity.

However, a Request for Admissions requires a response under oath, and if such a request is denied and is later proved to be wrong, the party who framed the Request for Admissions is entitled to recover from the opposing party all costs connected with proving that point.

If a party admits the genuineness of certain documents, those documents may be admitted into evidence without further foundation, subject only to their relevance to the issues in the lawsuit.

4) **"Request for Production of Documents and Other Things"** is made to enable the opposing party to copy or photocopy them, to test them (usually in the case of defective products), or to otherwise see and examine the originals.

As with all other discovery tools, these requests are limited by their relevance to the subject matter of the lawsuit, their reasonable tendency to lead to the discovery of admissible evidence, or other rules of law which would preclude their having to be produced.

5) **"Request for Medical Examination, Mental Examination, Production of Items for Testing,"** etc., are pretty much self-explanatory. These discovery tools are used when someone's physical or mental condition is at issue, or when one side wants to test a certain item (such as a ladder) for defects that led to an incident causing injuries..

6) **"Request for Exchange of Information regarding Expert Witnesses."**

It would be very simple if each side simply explained his or her side of the case to a judge or jury, and if the judge or jury used an independent expert in a given field to interpret the facts as they apply to the law in a case.

Alas, in our technologically-driven society, that practice has long since gone by the wayside. In every single case of any substance that I have ever tried, each side relied on "experts."

If someone is hurt in an accident, each side hires "experts"—physicians, chiropractors, health care providers—to explain to a jury why (from the plaintiff's side), the claimant is so seriously (and expensively) injured and why that claimant is entitled to recover an extraordinary amount of money; or (from the defendant's side), why the claimant is malingering or being overtreated, or why the incident in question was not a substantial causative factor in the claimant's injuries.

In the case of Owner vs. Builder, Barrister has hired several experts on behalf of the Owners:

a) At least one senior general contractor, usually one accustomed to testifying in the court system, as an expert on how long the job should have taken, how much it should have cost, etc.

b) A psychiatrist to describe the mental agonies Mary Owner went through as a result of the "unconscionable" delays.

c) At least one expert in each of the subcontractor trades.

Defensor, of course, has hired his own stable of expert witnesses (on Builder's dime, or, more realistically, on monies supplied by Builder's insurance carrier) to counteract the testimony of the Owners' expert witnesses.

A reasonable time before trial, each side must disclose to the other the identity of their experts and what reports, if any, they have rendered. As soon as that is determined, there is a new round of Depositions of the experts. But here there is a notable exception. Experts charge significantly more for their depositions than do lay witnesses. It is not uncommon for a medical practitioner to charge $1,000 for a half-day's deposition. While part of that sum must be paid by the party seeking the expert's deposition, other expenses incurred in getting the expert to the Deposition (and sometimes this can be prohibitively expensive, particularly when the expert resides in another part of the State) are borne by the party who hired that expert.

The discovery laws breed many needless court appearances over what a party must produce or what he need not produce, or questions that a party must answer or need not answer. Usually the lawyer seeking to avoid a discovery request argues as follows:

a) The request for information is needlessly burdensome, harassing and oppressive. (Are you starting to get the idea that **all** lawsuits are needlessly burdensome, harassing and oppressive?)

b) The request for information is vague and ambiguous in that the lawyer cannot decipher exactly what it is that the party seeking information wants. (This from a profession that drafts and is supposed to be able to understand complex, arcanely worded statutes.)

c) The request for information invades the attorney's "work product." (How in the world do you tell what is "work product" and what is evidence that was there at the beginning?)

d) The request for information is too broad.

e) The request for information is not relevant to the subject matter of the lawsuit and not reasonably calculated to lead to the discovery of admissible evidence.

f) The request for information invades the attorney-client privilege.

Discovery statutes constitute a law unto themselves and might well be called "The Lawyer's Full Employment Act."

All this adds up to more out-of-pocket money for the luckless client.

Under the current legal system as practiced, the discovery process usually consumes the better part of six months or more, and but for the trial itself constitute by far the bulk of attorneys' fees and costs that the client will pay. And woe be to the lawyer who doesn't do all the discovery he's supposed to do. If the case is lost because of a lack of proper discovery, there's always another lawyer waiting in the wings to sue Barrister for legal malpractice.

Returning to the Owners' relatively simple case, by the time the pleadings have been settled and Discovery has been completed, two more years have gone by. The Owners have not only used up their original $10,000 retainer fee, but they are in debt to Barrister for another $10,000 in attorney's fees plus $5,000 in costs.

Now, one party or the other files a paper to get the case onto the Court's calendar for resolution. This paper is usually called something like an At-Issue Memorandum or Memorandum to Set Case for Trial. The opposing parties have 10-15 days, to file a Counter At-Issue Memorandum, which may set forth a series of unavailable dates for that party or his counsel, or which may argue that the case is not "at issue" (i.e. all the issues and parties have not been joined) and hence not ready for trial.

Irrespective of whether the At-Issue Memorandum is accepted as is or is challenged, the very first thing a Court will usually do is refer the matter to Judicial Arbitration. This usually takes place within 90-150 days after the At-Issue Memorandum is filed, and constitutes a "mini-trial."

Usually an attorney with several years of experience acts as the designated arbitrator.

If the arbitration were binding and had teeth, it would probably be an effective tool for alternative dispute resolution.

However, the way the laws are currently written, mandatory binding arbitration would deprive a litigant of his or her right to a jury trial. Thus, either side or any side can, for no reason at all, reject the arbitrator's award, in which case all parties return to the Court for calendar assignment and trial setting.

By now, if you're counting, it is 2½ years and some $25,000 after the Owners filed their lawsuit against Builder. Positions have crystallized. Even the poor Owners are not sure exactly what happened anymore. To make matters worse, they have become disgusted with the entire house and would just as soon sell it and move. But Barrister tells them that that could prejudice their case.

At the trial setting conference, the court orders Owner, Builder, and the rest of the parties, to attend a Mandatory Settlement Conference, usually six months later.

Almost three years to the day after they have filed their lawsuit—nearly four years after the fiasco of the building addition— the Owners, Builder and the subcontractors appear for settlement conference.

In many counties, properly handled, the settlement conference can be of great benefit to the parties, at least in theory. But alas, in practice, the settlement conference judge is usually so overburdened with his caseload that he can give the parties no more than an hour to explore settlement possibilities. Most of the time, the overworked judge has had no time to read the file and barely ten minutes to glance over the abbreviated Settlement Conference Statements prepared by the Attorneys.

All too often, the tired judge will ask the attorneys, "Well? Can you settle this case?" and when he hears the perfunctory, "No, Your Honor," he refers the case back to the master calendar department.

In master calendar, the Owners are finally given a definite, locked-in-concrete trial date, sixty days hence. They are among the fortunate, for they know that their case will be tried 3¼ years after they filed it.

Now the parties engage in last-minute trial preparation and posturing. Experts are formally retained and notified of the time and day they will be needed. The Owners are now told they must advance $2,500 for each of their expert witnesses. Other witnesses and records are subpoenaed. The case is now in the home stretch, right?

Wrong.

On the last day they are allowed to do so, Builder's lawyers file a Motion for Summary Judgment. This is a tactical maneuver, rarely granted, that may dispose of the case on a legal technicality, or a failure of the other side to produce a small, but necessary, element of its case.

Motions for Summary Judgment cost a lot of time and money to file and to defend. Even though they are virtually never granted, they constitute an excellent way to drive up fees yet again. Fortunately, the Motion for Summary Judgment filed by Builder's lawyer does not force a postponement in the trial date. The motion is denied, but only after the Owners have incurred an additional $2,000 in lawyer's fees to defeat it.

Now comes the day of reckoning: the date formally set for trial. The Owners, dressed in their best, sit across the courtroom glaring at Builder, while Builder in turn glares daggers at his subcontractors.

There are at least ten other plaintiffs and defendants in the courtroom as the judge calls the calendar. Finally he intones, "Case Number M216788, Arthur Owner and Mary Owner, Plaintiffs, versus Robert Builder, Defendant, and related cross-actions."

The lawyers jump up and each in turn says, "Ready, Your Honor."

"Gentlemen," the judge says solemnly, "I'm afraid we don't have a court available for you this morning. We have too many cases older than yours ahead of you. You can either trail calendar or we can re-set the case."

The term "trail calendar" is a killer in the legal profession. That means the lawyers and litigants wait on pins and needles for a courtroom to open up. Since each court usually has a weekly calendar call, it means that if you don't "go out" within the week you're called, you come back to the master calendar section the following week and your case is re-set for a new trial date, usually 60 to 90 days away.

A few years ago, in a medium-sized California county, I had a case called for trial. Then it was put on the "trial calendar," only to be re-set **eight consecutive times**. When the case ultimately went out to a jury for trial, it was fifteen months after the original court date. And to show the manifest breakdown of the system, after seven days of jury trial, which took 2½ weeks because of the court's other daily matters, the plaintiff, who had sued my client for "$265,000 plus punitive damages," settled the case for $3,000.

The nightmare does not end when the case finally gets to trial. The judge who tries the case rarely can devote an entire day to the trial. He or she usually has "grist" in the morning. That is the judge's "short" calendar, which usually consists of a mixed bag of criminal arraignments, default or uncontested divorce hearings and perhaps short law and motion matters.

Trial in the Owners' case usually will not start much before ten in the morning. There is one fifteen-minute break in the morning, a 1½-hour lunch, a fifteen-minute break in the afternoon, and court hearings usually don't go much past four o'clock. Out of a typical trial day, the Owners will be fortunate to get in four hours of actual trial. But since Barrister has cleared his calendar for the entire day, and since Barrister is actually at court from 8:30 A.M. until 4:30 P.M., Owner is billed for an entire day's work, plus, undoubtedly, the time that Barrister has devoted to reviewing the previous day's proceedings and preparing for the present day's hearing.

By this time, the Owners realize there is no way they can win, even if they "win."

If there is insurance—and most businesses do carry liability insurance—Builder doesn't care. He hasn't paid a cent. His lawyer's fees and costs are paid for by the insurance company. Being party to litigation is a pain in the neck for Builder, but it's certainly not the pain in the pocketbook that it is for Owner.

On the other hand, if Builder is a small businessman and the potential for recovery is large enough, he may very well consider filing bankruptcy if the verdict is substantial, and Owner will still get nothing, for the debt will most likely be discharged in bankruptcy.

Let's get back to what long ago became the Owners' worst nightmare.

Assume that the Owners have demanded a trial by jury. They must advance jury fees, usually $200 a day, and the court reporter's fee (about the same).

The first thing that happens, even before a jury is selected, is that the judge calls all of the lawyers—he calls them "Counsel"— into his chambers. While the Owners sit nervously wondering what is going on, the judge and the lawyers meet privately. The judge attempts to do some good old-fashioned arm-twisting and horse-trading to try to get the case settled. After all, the presiding judge is breathing down his neck to get rid of as many cases as possible so that the statistical record looks good.

The judge tells each side the same things they've heard a hundred times before: how the system is so crowded with needless cases that should have been settled; how each party can save a great deal of money by settling; how the uncertainties of trial can be avoided.

He then asks the various defense counsel to leave the room so he can speak privately with Barrister for a few moments. Once alone, the judge advises Barrister that the Owners could very easily lose the case and end up paying not only their own attorney's fees and costs, but Defensor's costs as well; that juries do strange things (Don't we lawyers know *that!*); that he may have to make some difficult evidentiary rulings that will harm the Owners' chances; and that the Owners should consider the common sense of settling. He then asks Barrister to give his "bottom line" figure, one which Barrister is prepared to recommend to his clients.

After the judge asks Barrister to step out of his chambers for a few moments to think about it, he invites the defense counsel back in. His Honor then advises the defense lawyers that they could easily lose the case and have to come in with "big bucks;" that it makes sense that since there are so many defendants and cross-defendants, their insurance companies should throw in a little something to get this case settled.

The lawyers for each defendant shrug, do a bit of finger-pointing, and say they'll discuss it. Ninety percent of all cases filed are ultimately settled before they reach this stage. Another 9½ percent are settled at this stage—you've heard the phrase "settled on the courthouse steps."

Almost invariably no litigant feels he has won anything. Each side grumbles about how much he or she has lost. Over the years, courts and lawyers have adopted the cynical adage: "A good settlement is one in which each party is equally unhappy with the result."

Not a great commentary on our legal system.

That is not to say there are many cases that do not get settled early in the game, or that you will find unconscionable delays in every court. In my home county of Monterey, cases regularly come to trial and are dispensed with quickly, and, I feel, fairly. Even in larger counties, I have seen cases be filed, go through an expedited, cooperative process, and come to trial and decision within eight or nine months. They are the exceptions to the rule. They have become increasingly rare as my years in practice have added up.

What I have described above is far more typical of what occurs in a trial situation—and far more tragic.

Let us return to the case of the Owners vs. Builder.

The lawyers return to chambers. Between Builder and his subcontractors, they have raised a grand total of $20,000 to "get rid of the case for nuisance value."

The judge nudges them up to $25,000, then tells Barrister that he doubts if the Owners will do any better at trial. At the very least they knew they were going to pay $60,000 for the addition. They financed $70,000 so they probably expected to go a little over budget. Change orders are a way of life and no contract ever goes quite right. They paid $84,000 and Builder says they owe him $25,000 more. That comes to $109,000. Builder's "side" is willing to waive the extra $25,000 and throw in another $25,000. That makes a net recovery to the Owners of $50,000. If they deduct $50,000 from $109,000, they'll end up with $59,000, which puts the Owners in exactly the same place they'd be if everything had gone as it was supposed to—heck, they actually come out $1,000 **ahead.**

Barrister halfheartedly argues about the attorney's fees, the delays and Mary Owner's nervous breakdown, not to mention that four years later the house is still not complete.

The judge patiently explains something Barrister already knows: there isn't an attorney's fee clause in the contract and the Owners cannot expect to recover fees. Barrister acknowledges that is so. The judge pontificates that delays are a fact of life and that it took far longer to get to this point than if the Owners had simply let Builder finish the addition. He does not feel a few months' delay was all that dramatic.

Barrister concedes that point, but raises the issue of mental aggravation.

The judge points to several pictures of his wife and grown children, indicating that he's a family man himself and there's lots of mental aggravation in life. It's not as though Builder deliberately set out to ruin Mary Owner's life. These things happen. How does Barrister propose to prove that Builder knew the plumber would go under after taking the money? The judge warns that Defensor will surely go through Mary Owner's whole background, picking apart the scabs of her life. She'd suffer more from that than she did from the delay. The judge then asks how much it would cost to complete the house.

Barrister responds it will cost another eight or nine thousand dollars.

"OK, say ten. Say eleven if it makes your clients happy. They get the addition for seventy thousand dollars. That's exactly the loan the Owners took out. So where are their damages?"

At this point, we draw away from this *Alice in Wonderland* reasoning. To the judge and to the lawyer, everything the judge says makes perfectly good sense. It is logically correct if you use the pettifogging logic that lawyers learn in law school and with which they are ingrained throughout their practice. It is a lawyer's way of coming to a logical, common sense conclusion. The only problem is that it simply does not achieve a fair result. The law is supposed to compensate a victim for all damages proximately caused by the wrong of another. But the term "all" as used by lawyers and judges seems to be a relative term.

After several more minutes of discussion, punctuated by the lawyers and the judge exchanging "war stories" of trials and times gone by, Barrister meets with the Owners and has a long discussion with them. Regardless of the impression that lawyers give their clients, when it comes down to pay dirt, lawyers really don't like to litigate.

That's because at bedrock most lawyers are not inherent-risk takers. They like to see things arranged in a predictable, orderly fashion. Trial lawyers on both sides of an issue have a pretty good idea what "predictable" and "orderly" mean in terms of judges and juries—the most unpredictable element in the trial game—by referring to publications such as *Jury Verdicts Weekly*, or such other periodicals, which advise lawyers about a majority of the reported jury verdicts in a given jurisdiction for any period of time. In addition to the publications, the various plaintiff's and defendant's trial lawyer organizations maintain up-to-date computer records of the results of virtually every trial that goes to decision in the United States.

Thus, if an offer is "reasonable"—and an offer encouraged by the judge as reasonable is usually accepted by the lawyer as reasonable—it is in the lawyer's best interest to sell that settlement to the client. After all, the lawyer will almost certainly have to appear before that judge again, and he doesn't want to be thought of as someone who makes waves.

By this time, the lawyer has pretty well milked the case for the maximum fee he is going to get. He has a pretty good idea of what the judge thinks should happen in the case. There's not going to be that much more in fees, and if the client loses, the lawyer is going to have trouble collecting the extra money anyway.

So once the lawyer is convinced that the offer is "in the ballpark," he will usually apply his persuasive skills not to the jury, but to getting his client to settle.

Now it's time for Barrister to sell the settlement to his clients First he lays out the details of the proposed settlement to his stunned clients, and has already started to "soften them up."

Then he begins a one-person "Mutt and Jeff," or "good-cop/bad cop" routine, telling them not to get him wrong; if they say no to this settlement offer, they'll never hear anything more about it from him again and he'll happily try the case. It's their money, after all, and they can do with it what they want.

(This is not quite a true statement. The Owners will hear about the settlement offer throughout the trial, and if they get a less favorable verdict, the lawyer can justify his position by saying he tried to tell them they had a very good offer and should have taken it.)

But, the Owners say unhappily, they're losing everything. They're worse off than when they started.

Not at all, says Barrister. What did they have when they started? Eighty-four thousand dollars that they had already paid, plus exposure (a favorite lawyer word) to another $25,000. He tells them they're getting an absolute windfall here. He should think they'd be thankful that he was able to engineer this deal. They wouldn't believe how he had to push the other side around to get this offer. But again, he wants them to know that he is not trying to force them into anything. If the case goes to trial, it will cost them another $2,000 a day in fees, plus costs. Let's assume the case will take a week to try. That's $14,000 and, he reminds them, he told them at the beginning there are no attorney's fees at the end of the rainbow for them. Win, lose or draw, they are responsible for their own fees..

But, Art Owner says helplessly, Builder will be paying his fees, too. He should want to throw something in to avoid the expense and embarrassment to himself.

Barrister now tells his clients that this is not clear thinking. Builder doesn't care whether he gets whacked with a judgment or not. It's all insurance money. So he misses a few days' work. Big deal. His crews go out and do the work. He's not paying any fees.

So, Owner says, there's really no incentive for him to settle? Barrister responds "None at all." When the Owners sadly point out that they're still losing, Barrister says that while that may unfortunately be true, in the long run they can say they forced Builder into a settlement—unless, of course, he insists on a confidentiality clause.

A confidentiality clause?

Yes, that's something just about every defendant insists on today. If he buys his peace, he doesn't want anyone else to know about what happened. That's usually part of the settlement.

But, the Owners gasp, the world should know what a charlatan he is!

Barrister asks how that's going to help them. Is it going to make one bit of difference in their case?

The Owners tell their lawyer he sounds like he doesn't want to try their case. Barrister smoothly responds that he never said he didn't want to try it. After all, he's a trial lawyer, that's why they hired him. But, he reminds them, he's a counselor as well as an advocate, and his job is to counsel them to curb their losses, to get the maximum they can without risk

Risk? What risk? the Owners ask.

Barrister then tells them that if they get a judgment of one penny less than what Builder's side offered, the court can make them pay all of Builder's costs other than attorney's fees—such as depositions, experts' fees and jury fees. Barrister tells them he knows this has got to be hurting them, but it's hurting him, too, right in his pocketbook. He then offers that if everyone can get this case wound up and settled today, he—Barrister—is willing to throw in the fees he would charge them for today—$2,000.

When the Owners dejectedly ask Barrister's advice—should they settle or should they take the case to trial—Barrister responds (the most hypocritical statement of all) that he can't advise them what to do. He'll be content either way. It's their decision. It's a matter of how much more they want to spend and how much they think they'll get back in the end. That's up to them. He's seen juries go both ways. Appeals can take years and cost thousands of dollars. Don't forget, in addition to his fees, they must also advance experts' fees, jury fees, court reporter fees. He then suggests that what everyone is truly looking for is to bring the matter to a close so they can get on with their lives.

And so forth and so on. You get the picture? Barrister is playing "good cop/bad cop" all by himself. As for throwing in the day's attorney's fees, Barrister is not quite the altruist he portrays himself to be. If he gets back to his office before noon—or even if he gets back at 1:30 after a nice, leisurely lunch that will probably be paid for by the defense counsel as they start to "old soldier" the case, he will still have an afternoon full of ".2 hour" billing units that should more than make up for his "sacrifice."

Incidentally, what Barrister is doing is in no way frowned on by the bench or by the bar (lawyer words for the courts and other lawyers). It is looked upon as doing yeoman service to insure that the client's best interests are served and that justice is done in an orderly, predictable manner. We could go on with this story for the next several pages, but it would only become more depressing. The Owners are "damned if they settle, damned if they don't settle."

In one instance, Barrister is absolutely correct. Juries make strange, sometimes "off-the-wall" decisions based on absolutely incoherent reasoning.

Let's assume that, browbeaten and demoralized, the Owners settle the case for $25,000 plus waiver of the $25,000 Builder was claiming for overages. A month later, when they get the final bill from Barrister they figure out what it has cost them in monetary terms—never mind the mental aggravation, the time element, the misery and humiliation they were put through during their depositions, or the time they lost from their lives. Let's talk nothing but dollars and cents.

If things had gone as expected: $60,000, for which they would have had a completed addition, $70,000 at most.

As it finally developed:

Paid to Builder . . . .$ 84,000
Fees paid to Barrister: . . . .$ 30,000
   Depositions . . . .$ 4,500
   Photocopies . . . .$ 1,500
   Postage . . . .$ 500
   Doctor's Bill for Mary
     (80% paid by insurance,
     20% by owners) . . . .$ 1,200
   Doctor's retainer for court
     testimony (nonrefundable) . . . . .$ 1,500
   Contractor expert fees . . . .$ 5,000
   Total legal fees and costs   **$ 44,200**

Gross expenditure $128,200
Less payment from defendants . . . .(25,000)
Net out-of-pocket cost to the Owners: $103,000

The Owners probably could have settled with Builder early on by saying, "Look, we've paid you $84,000. We're not happy. You're not happy. Let's both simply walk away from the deal." That's not to say it would have been a good solution. But taking all things into consideration, it probably would have been a better solution than what finally happened.

When they brought this to the attention of Barrister, the lawyer sighed dramatically and said, "Yes, I guess you were right and I can see your point. But don't forget, since the lawyer's fees and costs were spent to protect your assets, you might be able to deduct them for tax purposes. That means that you really didn't pay $44,200, you really only paid about thirty-one thousand out of your own pocket. You'd have had to pay the rest in taxes anyway."

With typical "lawyer logic," that statement makes absolute sense.

And it is absolute nonsense.

As I said at the beginning of this chapter, Stephen King books are scary but fun. Lawsuits are scary and they're never fun.

CHAPTER 6

"Band-Aids on a Cancer": Why Proposed "Solutions" Won't Work

"Laws are generally found to be nets of such a texture as the little creep through, the great break through, and the middle size alone are entangled in."

– Shenstone

N RECENT YEARS, legislatures, "hearing the voice of the people," declared that no longer would there be interminable delays for justice. Most states have enacted laws that mandate every case will be tried within a certain time—usually two years after filing. The federal courts followed suit with their own trial delay reduction procedures, which, although they are as numerous and confusing as the number of district courts in the United States, attempt to carry out the noble purpose of swift, sure justice.

There is only one thing wrong with this wonderful goal: It won't work.

1) We don't have enough judges to hear all the cases in a reasonable time.

2) In every jurisdiction in America, criminal cases have precedence over the available court resources. Civil cases always "ride the back of the bus."

3) With constant pressure for tax reduction and the cutting of "waste" in government spending, we don't have the money to hire more judges.

4) A high percentage of excellent lawyers who would make outstanding judicial candidates can't afford to become judges because they have set a lifestyle commensurate with what they make as lawyers, and they would make far less once they were elevated to the bench.

But legislatures have enacted laws and the judges must obey them. Therefore, virtually every busy court in the country has enacted "Fast Track"—a full-employment program for large, well-financed law firms and a nightmare for every other practicing lawyer.

Although the format of "Fast Track" varies from jurisdiction to jurisdiction, an "average" fast-track calendar, which provides for a series of "case management conferences," will provide a schedule something like this:

Day	Event
1	File civil suit. Summons issued
60	Summons must be served or sanctions will issue
90	Answer must be filed for all served defendants
120	First case management conference
180	Set judicial arbitration/prehearing: 60 days
320	Set discovery cutoff: 200 days from conference
350	Set motion cutoff date: 230 days from conference
365	Set pre-trial conference: 245 days from conference
425	Mandatory settlement conference
455	Trial commences

On paper it looks great for the litigant. He knows that his case will come to trial eighteen months after he filed it. That's a far cry from the time the Owners waited for their trial with Builder.

But there is no such thing as "free," and all that speed comes at a very high price.

The average trial lawyer has a caseload at any given time of fifty to 100 active files. While an actor portraying a lawyer on TV may try major cases each week, in real life even the top trial lawyers rarely take more than two or three substantial cases to trial in a year.

In between those trials, that lawyer will have at least two law-and-motion matters a week, each of which requires time for preparation. He or she will spend on average four hours a week taking on new clients—a legitimate four hours, by the way, not the ".2" type of time. Telephone calls will be instituted and returned. The lawyer may have "short cause" trials, arbitration hearings, conferences; he or she will need to take several depositions in connection with caseload requirements; supervise younger lawyers if he or she has the good fortune to have such junior associates; take witness statements; dictate responses to letters; and, occasionally, take time off for lunch and to be with his or her family.

Lawyers also catch colds and the flu, have dental appointments and appointments with their accountants. They might even go shopping for their spouses. And being human—and engaged in an occupation that calls for top-level mental concentration most of the working day—they can only accomplish so much before the physical, mental, and emotional machinery breaks down.

With "Fast Track," the lawyer must work even harder and faster to meet the new deadlines. If he or she does not meet them, it is the lawyer, not the client, who suffers monetary sanctions.

Most lawyers who serve the vast bulk of Middle America operate from small firms. Large firms invariably serve the well-heeled clients, corporations, and insurance companies. Large firms benefit greatly from "Fast Track." They simply assign a "trial team" of two or three lawyers to each case—after all, the client will pay for it—and it's easy to explain that this is a necessity because of the new fast-track rules.

Where in days past, the smaller firm could budget its time because there was no limit on when discovery would end, now there is a finite—and often unreasonably short—time limit in which to complete discovery. It becomes particularly onerous when a small firm is handling many cases.

The immediate question you might ask is, "If it's so hard, why doesn't the lawyer simply take fewer cases and handle the ones he has more expeditiously?" The question sounds perfectly logical, but in practice it doesn't work like that.

If I had the time to do absolutely everything a lawyer is supposed to do to completely and perfectly bring a case to trial, the Owners in the last chapter would have had a bill of $142,000 rather than $42,000. How many clients do you think a lawyer could keep under those conditions, and for how long?

The answer to the dilemma is that a lawyer budgets his or her time to do the best possible work, given the time and money constraints imposed by the reality of the situation. That means, quite frankly, that in all but the largest cases for the largest clients, every lawyer cuts corners. That is not due to dishonesty, incompetence, or malpractice. It is simply a fact of life.

There are a few lawyers—statistically a minuscule number—who have unlimited funds to work with, who can assign an army of junior associates to grind out the work like so many sausages. But most of us don't have that luxury.

So what happens with "Fast Track"? One of two things. Either the lawyers understand that they'll have to cooperate fully and quickly with one another, and there is an agreement to exchange information informally and inexpensively—which is one of the goals "Fast Track" set out to accomplish. Or, as is too often the case, the large firms use the shortened discovery schedules to batter an opponent into submission.

Here's how the latter program works. We will use Owner's case as an example.

As soon as the Owners file their lawsuit, Builder, through his large insurance law firm, answers the complaint and immediately sends out a series of Interrogatories, Requests for Admissions, and Requests for Production of Documents—all due within thirty days. Barrister, who heads a small but busy firm, scurries to meet the production deadlines imposed by the court. He serves and files the best and most complete answers he can.

The Defensor law firm, contending that the Answers are not sufficient, regardless of whether they are or not, files a Motion to compel further responses to discovery requests, which requires Barrister to make a court appearance.

The motion is set for hearing. Barrister and Defensor trade reams of paper. On the day of the hearing, they come before Judge Overload, who tells them, "Counsel, I am sorry but I have no time to read all this paper or rule on discovery requests. Because of the Trial Delay Reduction Act, I must try at least one case every week and this simply doesn't give me the time or resources to rule on discovery motions. I will refer this out to retired Judge Berlin."

In many large cities, the courts have adopted this very policy. They will appoint a retired judge—a "private judge"—to act as discovery referee because they cannot spare "sitting" judges for anything but trials.

That sounds OK. After all, a retired judge was a judge, and it's not as though they're doddering in their dotage. So what's the big deal?

The big deal is that these retired judges don't work for free. They charge $300 or more per hour for their time and wisdom. And while the retired judge has the authority to dictate who is going to pay for his or her time, each side must initially divide the fee equally.

An active, sitting judge has very little time to look over the voluminous discovery pleadings. On the other hand, a retired judge, who is being paid by the hour, has all the time in the world to review them. It is not unusual for a retired judge to take the better part of a day studying the papers and preparing questions, the better part of an hour to hear the matter, and a substantial additional amount of time to hand down a decision.

There is nothing wrong with that practice, and in recent years a large number of judges have retired, to enable them to serve as "private judges." The decisions these judges make are usually better-thought-out and better written than decisions made when they were active sitting judges, for now they have the time they always needed.

The problem is that if, on average, the retired judge's fees are $2,000 and each side must pay half, the Owners end up paying an additional $1,000 for discovery rulings they did not instigate when, in older days and in smaller jurisdictions, that was something done for free by the sitting judge.

Take the reverse of the above situation. Barrister sends out a series of interrogatories. Builder's lawyers completely stonewall Barrister and give him nothing but skeleton information. When Barrister's earnest requests for answers fall on deaf ears, Barrister has only two alternatives:

1) He can simply do without information that he critically needs to avoid surprise at the time of trial; or
2) He can go into court and move for an order compelling further responses to discovery requests.

A friend of mine, an outstanding trial lawyer in Los Angeles, who asked that I not use his name, shared a recent experience with me when he brought a motion to compel responses to interrogatories in Los Angeles County Superior Court.

"My client was a middle-class working man who had suffered brain damage in an accident. I sent out a series of twenty interrogatories. The insurance firm objected or gave evasive Answers to fourteen of the questions. I had been through the Los Angeles court system before. They routinely assign discovery matters out to retired judges as referees at $300 per hour. My client simply didn't have the money to spend on this suit and the other side knew it.

"When we got to court that morning, I saw a small, hand-lettered sign that said, 'Equal access to justice begins here.' The judge had issued a 'tentative ruling' assigning the matter to a private judge for adjudication. When the judge came on the bench, I asked to be heard on the matter. I explained to the judge that this motion didn't involve a lot of questions or questions of great complexity, and my client could not afford to pay the proposed retired judge.

"The judge looked at me and said, 'Counsel, I sympathize with your problem but I have thirty-four matters on my law-and-motion calendar this morning. I simply don't have time to deal with them. I'm sorry, but that's a fact.'

"For a moment, I remained silent, considering whether what I wanted to say next would put me in contempt of court. But I knew I had to say it. 'Your Honor,' I replied. 'The sign in your courtroom says, 'Equal access to justice begins here.' There is no way my client can afford what you are ordering him to do. If that is the way you are going to rule, you might as well turn that sign upside down or take it off your wall, because it has no meaning to someone like my client.'

"The judge sighed as though he had heard it all before and said, 'Counsel, there is nothing I can do about it. I simply don't have the time and that's the way it is. Case is assigned to retired Judge Jones.' "

Of course one can argue that it's a "cost" of litigation and the prevailing party will "win" that money back at the end of the case. But as we have seen in the case of Owner vs. Builder, cases almost invariably settle with each side paying its own attorneys' fees and costs.

There is no question that "Fast Track" has made litigation more costly for the little person, and is heavily weighted in favor of the large firms.

Another recent development in jurisprudence has been the rise of private trials—the so-called "rent-a-judge" program. For those who can afford it, it has resulted in faster, smoother, far more efficient trials. It is like being able to drive in the "car pool" lane of the freeway—virtually no congestion, full speed ahead. There are only two things wrong with rent-a-judge:

1) While it works very well for the rich, it denies equal justice to the rest of us. The rent-a-judge, usually a retired trial or appeals court judge—charges an average of $300 per hour for his or her time. The parties usually divide the cost of the private judge, and the judge may or may not rule that one party ultimately has to pay all of his fees. In a ten-day trial, the judge's fees can run to $25,000. That's a lot of money for a system where there is supposed to be "equal justice for all."

2) Second, the rise of the rent-a-judge system has deprived the active, sitting bench of some of its brightest, and certainly its most popular, stars. In most states, a judge may retire at full pay after he or she has served on the bench for a certain

number of years, usually between ten and twenty, or when he or she reaches a certain age.

Contrary to popular belief, a trial judge does not become a wealthy man from being elevated to the bench. A salary of $80,000 to $100,000 per year is not uncommon. Granted, that's more than most of us make, but that's before taxes, Social Security, withholding for the judges' retirement fund, and numerous other deductions.

Doctors, lawyers, or businessmen in every walk of life have little things they can to do lessen the tax impact: things like taking a client or customer to lunch (entertainment expense) or other costs of doing business. Not so the judge. The judge cannot legally deduct **any** business expenses because he or she is a public servant. Thus the judge does not have the right to take "expenses" that some of us write off. In smaller businesses, there exists—whether we want to admit it or not—a "gray" market where a certain amount of cash income is passed "under the table" and is not declared for tax purposes. Judges are paid out of county budgets, and it's all reported.

One morning, a 62-year-old judge who's been sitting on the bench for twenty years, realizes that he can retire from the active judiciary, draw his retirement, and earn $300 an hour working as a private judge instead of the $65 an hour he earns on the bench. By that time, his children are in graduate school. He has many deferred bills to pay. He's been promising his wife a trip to Europe for years, but because judges aren't supposed to be gone for longer than ten days at a time, he's never been able to take her. He still has his health, and, in today's society, he is young and vigorous.

He also knows that sitting as a private rent-a-judge is much, much easier than sitting on the public court. The class of litigants is higher, the lawyers are generally more reasonable, the atmosphere is genteel, you don't have to go to the most dangerous part of a downtown metropolitan area each day, and the opportunities for a pleasant judicial experience are much greater than in the inner city.

Small wonder so many judges elect to take early retirement and become private judges. The decision is made even easier by the fact that there now exist services such as JAMS (Judicial Arbitration and Mediation Service) that do all the administrative tasks for the judge and even find work for the retired judge. Even with rent-a-judges, however, all is not equal. The judge who was a martinet on the public bench, or who treated people shabbily, will not be in demand nearly as much as the one who always treated lawyers and clients with dignity and respect, who had a good "judicial temperament," and who was known as a careful, thoughtful jurist.

The mean-spirited judge who lacks compassion, who found himself unpopular among members of the bar during his tenure as judge, knows that his pickings as a private judge will be slim, so he remains on the public bench, perhaps longer than he should. The rent-a-judge system points out in capital letters the difference between wealthy litigants and "the rest of us."

Although somewhat belatedly, most courts have now concluded that some form of alternative dispute resolution is necessary, both to alleviate court congestion and to act as a catalyst for meaningful settlement negotiations.

In our calendar model, set forth above, the judicially appointed arbitration hearing takes place within six months of the filing of the lawsuit, usually before each side has engaged in substantial and expensive discovery. That is a salutary sign. Usually the court appoints arbitrators from the more senior members of the local bar. Those arbitrators have agreed in advance to accept a certain, relatively nominal amount to act as arbitrator. On the one hand, that is good because it truly does afford every litigant a free prehearing judge. On the other hand, because of the reduced, "piecework" fee, a lawyer-arbitrator isn't going to devote a great deal of time to the arbitration when he has more lucrative work waiting.

Arbitration is akin to a trial. However, the rules of evidence are usually relaxed, the atmosphere is much less formal than in a trial, and the arbitrator's primary aim is to avoid the peripheral matters and get to the heart of the case. The arbitrator may question witnesses, make observations on the evidence presented during the hearing, conduct independent settlement conferences with the lawyers and their clients after calling a break in the hearings, and will usually render a written opinion.

Arbitration is good for another reason: a litigant with unreasonable expectations may have a glass of cold judicial water splashed in his face when a purportedly independent, neutral listener hears evidence and arguments and issues a presumably thoughtful, fair decision.

But judicial arbitration is not binding. Any party may reject the arbitration award within a set time—usually thirty days—after it is handed down. If that occurs, the arbitration is void—as though it had never been—except that the litigants have now paid additional lawyers' fees and, in some cases, expert witness fees, to ride a train on a track to nowhere.

To circumvent the specter of costly trials and inherent delays, many contracts today provide for binding arbitration. Almost every hospital in the United States has an arbitration clause concerning disputes that arise when a patient is in the hospital. Fortunately, laws in every state provide that a patient has a certain amount of time after surgery or treatment to reject the arbitration clause.

The critical words in the contract are "**binding** arbitration." Courts will invariably throw a case out of court and send it to binding arbitration if the parties have agreed in the contract upon that means of dispute resolution, unless both sides agree to waive arbitration and proceed to trial.

Binding arbitration has its good points and its bad points. First the good:

1) The hearing and the decision are generally informal, swift, and certain.
2) There is an inherent cost savings because arbitration does not usually use the lengthy discovery system employed by the courts. You get your hearing, you get your decision.

Then the not-so-good:

1) Arbitrators are not bound by law. Unless the arbitrators are part of a large, organized service, such as American

Arbitration Association, JAMS, U.S. Arbitration and Mediation Service, National Association of Securities Dealers securities arbitration, etc., they can set any procedure they want, when and as they want.

2) Arbitrators can make any decision they want. They need not give either participant the reasoning behind their decision. They can hand down as simple a decision as "Decision in favor of John Jones, $25,000." That is all they need to do.

3) The arbitration award is binding. There is no right to a jury. Often, there may not be a fair opportunity for cross-examination. A court will not look behind the reasoning of the award. A court will not set aside the award in the absence of provable fraud. An utter mistake in the law does not furnish grounds for reversal, even if the award is totally absurd. There is no right of appeal to any court. There is no such thing as fair or unfair. The award is final. Period. While the result may be certain, it is not necessarily "justice."

The most honest hope when it comes to true problem-solving is mediation. Although current mediation attempts suffer from the fact that many of them are conducted by retired judges and other types who are accustomed to the decision-making rather than the problem-solving process, I believe this is the best means of achieving justice in its truest sense.

But to get to that point, we have a long way to go. We must fight established interests—lawyers and insurance companies, who resist any change from the way things are done now. To get there will require nothing less than a revolution in American thought, the dismemberment of the old beliefs of what should work, and the demand of the market that lawyers finally follow what the public wants them to do and not what they think is best for the public.

We Must Change the Way We Think— We Must Reclaim Control of Our Legal Rights

A doctor and a lawyer were arguing at a cocktail party. "I do ten operations a day," boasted the doctor. "I've perfected my technique so that every operation is successful. You, on the other hand, try cases and advise clients in a very imprecise manner. What do you have to say for yourself about that?"

"You're absolutely right. In my field, my practice does not make me perfect. It just makes me rich."

THUS FAR, WE HAVE TALKED about what's wrong with lawyers and what's wrong with the system. It's easy to blame someone else or something else for your own troubles. It's harder to say, "We—all of us—created this problem. Now it's up to us to solve the problem."

What I propose is nothing less than that we rethink the way our society deals with its problems, change our perception, and then change the practice.

Can it be done? Of course. There have been numerous milestones in man's history far more profound than changing a legal system. Before Abraham, the idea of ethical monotheism, of one God and responsibility for one's own acts, was "off the wall." In the Middle Ages, scientific inquiry came to a relative halt in

Europe as mankind adhered to the Age of Faith. People changed. The flat world became the globe we know today. When Copernicus asked the heretical question, "Sun, stand Thou still?" we reversed the entire way we thought of the universe.

Within the past century alone, we have come further technologically than in the previous five million years. The concept of representative democracy took root and flourished; political communism lived and died. We can go from one side of our country to another, not in the several months it took 150 years ago, but in less than seven hours. There is no reason on earth why we cannot, with education, good will and a slight alteration of our mental perceptions, change the way we dispense justice in our society. It begins with each of us.

Let's start over with Owner's and Builder's dispute of a few chapters back. Time has gone by. Tempers and stresses have somewhat diminished. The Owners have gone to visit Barrister and received the diagnosis of what happens next. Instead of signing Barrister's contract, the Owners say they'll think about it for a day. Art Owner's next stop is Builder's office. Builder is no happier to see Owner than Owner is to see Builder, but they can't avoid one another. The initial conversation is strained, but after a while it takes the following direction:

Owner says he knows Builder is upset. You'd better believe he (Owner) is upset. Owner tells Builder he's just been to his lawyer's office. Builder, outraged at Owner's implied threat, doesn't even want to talk to Owner, since he believes Owner will twist anything he says, against him.

Owner asks Builder to hear him out. Owner says they can always go to the lawyers if they have to. He's just suggesting that before they start the battle, they should look at the whole situation. He asks Builder if he has any idea how much a lawyer costs. Builder replies that a lawyer costs a bundle, and every time something happens, his insurance rates go through the roof.

Owner tells Builder that Barrister has told him it could run a few thousand dollars, and neither party would get the fees back from the other because there's nothing in the contract about the winning party getting fees. Builder's lawyer told him the same thing. He laments that he's been after his lawyer to write an attorney's fee clause into his contracts for years, but the lawyer says that if he does that, people will sue him more often, and in the end he'll only lose.

Owner says sometimes he thinks the law really sucks. Builder agrees. Owner, smiling for the first time, says at least they agree on something. He points out that the two of them started out as friends. They were going to do a project together that would have made money for Builder and would have gotten Owner's addition built. Things didn't work out the way either of them wanted.

Builder, heating up, says it's not his fault. The electrician, the....

At this point, Owner interrupts him. Maybe that's the whole problem. They've both been looking to find fault and gear up for a big legal fight. There's got to be some graceful way to extricate themselves from this mess.

Builder claims he's got subcontractors and material providers to pay, and he feels bad enough about what happened that he's done this last part of the contract for Owner at cost.

Owner does not try to dissuade Builder from his feelings. But, he says, if *he* starts by telling Builder he expected to get into this house for $60,000 and he's already got $84,000 into it, that will get the parties nowhere. They both know they're in a bad spot. There's got to be a way they can work it out. Perhaps they should talk to the subcontractors and material providers and make them part of the solution.

Owner continues: "If we start with the idea that we want to solve this without the courts and without the thousands of dollars of lawyer's fees we'd both spend, we should be able to think of something." Owner says he's read about federal mediators helping unions and companies to get together. "Maybe there's some third person who's not so close to this problem who could help us come up with new ideas. After all, we know two things already: there's only so much money around and only so much house addition that has to be finished."

Builder adds that if they don't get things settled, the only people who'll end up happy are the lawyers.

Owner says, "So we agree on two things: no courts and no lawyers if we can avoid it."

At this point, Owner and Builder have turned a very significant corner in their thinking. They have abandoned the age-old notion—one that is not prevalent in every society, by the way—that the best way to settle a dispute is through adversarial proceedings.

If we multiplied that way of thinking to every field where we currently resolve things through the court system, the practice of law would shrink to its necessary best size. Those who would be drawn into the legal field by the promise of power and fortune would turn elsewhere, and the percentage of lawyers in our society would fall to a reasonable number, such as exist in most other civilized nations of the world.

Regardless of the nature of any civil dispute, there are three basic rules on which I believe we should all be able to agree:

A) Everyone wants to do that which is in his or her own best interests.

B) Everyone defines what his or her best interests are; no one has the power to tell another person what is in that person's best interests.

C) Everyone would like to keep as much power to himself or herself as possible, and would like to give away as little power as possible.

If you agree with these three statements, you have come 90 percent of the way toward changing the way in which you—and our society—think, and we are well on the way toward an honest, society-wide reform in the way we resolve problems.

Perhaps your first thought echoes mine: that the proposed solution is so simplistic, so naive, that it can't possibly work. You might be right, but remember: we're not talking about the details yet. We are talking basic concepts, skeletons on which we'll construct a body as we go along. Let's explore each of these three concepts in detail to see where they lead.

A) **Everyone wants to do that which is in his or her own best interests.** We define and redefine our own "best interests" a hundred times a day. In running our everyday lives, many of those decisions are spur-of-the-moment and don't take a great deal of concentrated effort. When we expand the "best interests" philosophy into the realm of human dispute, we also define and redefine what we mean.

Not everything that makes us angry results in litigation. I have been uncomfortable with something my son, daughter, or wife has done on more occasions than I care to count. Sometimes I give vent to my feelings. Sometimes I decide to be "a little nearsighted" or "a little hard of hearing," not because I need to pacify or capitulate, but because, in the grand scheme of my life, the dispute is not all that important, and I know that things will ultimately come into balance.

A few years ago, my neighbor and I had a misunderstanding concerning whether or not we would spend Thanksgiving together. There was a momentary hurt and we actually had difficulty speaking to one another for a couple of days. Then we found a graceful, humor-filled way out of the morass, and things came back into balance.

Let's return to the Owner versus Builder situation again. Initially, Owner believes that his best interests include the following:

1. To punish Builder.
2. To dominate what he perceives as Builder's control of the situation.
3. To make Builder's life as uncomfortable as he feels Builder has made his life.
4. To force Builder to his (Owner's) way of thinking.
5. To get Builder publicly to admit that he was wrong.
6. To humiliate Builder.
7. To force Builder to finish his house addition now.
8. To avoid paying Builder anything more.
9. To teach Builder a lesson not to mess with him.
10. To earn Mary's respect when he teaches Builder a lesson.

11. To redeem his own self-esteem and feel that he hasn't been made a fool and a dupe.
12. To get Builder to give him back the excess money he paid.
13. To have as much power over Builder as possible.
14. To drive Builder out of town.
15. To bankrupt Builder.

Whether we agree or not, to Owner these are very legitimate and immediate perceptions of his best interests. In one form or another, each of us has had the same emotional feelings in similar situations.

The perspective from Builder's side is somewhat different. Given his own anger, Builder perceives **his** own best interests to include the following:

1. Getting that deadbeat flake Owner to pay his justly due bill.
2. Getting that stupid man to realize that nothing is perfect in this world and that it's not his fault that the subcontractors didn't do their jobs.
3. Getting Owner to realize that his wife made so many changes that he (Builder) couldn't possibly afford to build the addition for $60,000—it's all her fault.
4. To punish Owner for making life so hard for him.
5. To make Owner's life as uncomfortable as he feels Owner has made his life.
6. To force Owner to his (Builder's) way of thinking.
7. To get Owner publicly to admit that he was wrong.
8. To humiliate Owner.
9. To teach Owner a lesson not to mess with him.
10. To fight for his business's honor.
11. To redeem his own self-esteem and feel that he hasn't been made a fool and a dupe.
12. To have as much power over Owner as possible.
13. To drive Owner out of town.
14. To force the subcontractors and material providers to own up to their responsibility in this mess.

One might think there is no way these differences can end up except in the courts, or, half-jokingly, with one side taking out a "contract" on the other. But once we get beyond the initial feelings of anger, frustration, betrayal and hurt, we realize that neither Owner nor Builder can realistically expect to drive the other out of town, or to bring the other around to his exact way of thinking. A court isn't going to achieve that end, and both Owner and Builder know it. Likewise, neither party is going to get the other to admit that he was wrong. So we're left with letting each party redefine his initial concept of what is in his own best interests.

Are there any points on which the two warriors, Owner and Builder, can agree? There probably are. Let's get to the easiest one: Spending $30,000 each on lawyers' fees is neither in Builder's nor Owner's best interests. Even if Builder's insurance covers the attorneys' fees and costs, his insurance premiums will go up and his reputation will be hurt.

A corollary of that point is: Going to court is not in anyone's best interest if the parties can somehow resolve their differences. Once Owner and Builder have somehow communicated these ideas to one another, they've taken a healthy step toward **constructively** identifying and resolving the problem. Once Owner and Builder decide they would each spend, at a minimum, $25,000 on attorneys' fees, they have a $50,000 pot with which to work. That is not to say that Owner wants to pay a nickel of that sum to Builder or that Builder intends to take a nickel less on what he believes he is owed. It simply means that there is an untapped pool of money that neither believed was there, that is now available.

In their initial preparations for warfare, this thought never even entered either of their minds. When Owner and Builder temporarily put their weapons and their first perceptions of their own best interests aside, each can concentrate on what he really wants.

Owner wants his addition completed as soon as possible and he doesn't want to pay any more than he's already paid. For the first time, he thinks, "I've already paid $84,000, which is $24,000 more than I thought I'd have to pay. Since I borrowed $70,000, it's really only $14,000 more than I had planned to pay. That money's already gone. If Builder will finish up my house, he can keep the extra money and choke on it."

Builder starts to contemplate. "The job's been mucked up and there's nothing much I can do about it. The plumber owes me a big favor from another job, and I can probably make it up to him on the next job. If I get him to throw in some labor by telling him I won't chase him on this job, that ought to convince him. Same with the masonry subcontractor. What'll it **really** cost me, bottom line, to finish it? If I do it myself, we can get it done over the weekend. It'll cost me about $5,000, but this job's already a loser and I made some money on the front end. Some of the subs'll just have to eat it on this job. The more of us there are to shoulder the burden, the less we'll each have to pay. Besides, Owner has already paid me $24,000 more than he thought it was going to cost him."

That's not to say that such simplistic thinking will, or even should, occur so early in the process. What is critically important is that the two sides are each thinking in terms of options and alternatives, flexibility rather than crystallization. In such an atmosphere problems can be constructively solved if each side goes one more extra step.

"You know, Builder," Owner suggests. "Maybe we could get someone at the trades council, someone we both trust, to help us put a value on what this should have cost?"

"That might not be a bad idea," Builder responds. "But that could get awfully public and I have to live in this town. What about if we went out of town and agreed to keep this quiet?"

"I don't mind doing that if it's going to help us resolve things. I've got another idea. The past is the past. We're not going to be able to change it. Why don't we move forward from here, since each of us has a different opinion of why we're here now?"

Although I have taken a classic mediator's reasoning statement and put it into one party's mouth, both parties will eventually have to come to the conclusion that "We're in this together. We can't go backward and establish 'facts' that each of us sees from a different perspective. We're here now and we must move forward from here to resolve a dispute that exists now."

This brief illustration shows how a change in the perception of what is in our own best interests—a willingness to move to a different part of the globe to get a different "world view"—is essential if we are going to resolve problems constructively, without the unnecessary intervention of courts or lawyers.

Note that I said "without the *unnecessary* intervention of courts or lawyers." While there will undoubtedly be some problems where parties conclude that they must ultimately go to court to achieve their "own best interests," this number can be reduced to almost zero if parties are willing to rethink and redefine their perceptions.

B) The second basic rule in constructive problem resolution is the ultimate realization that **each person defines for himself or herself what his or her own best interests are.** No one has the right or the power to tell another person what is in his or her best interests.

Whenever I hear or make that statement, I can't help but smile as I remember a classic scene from the Woody Allen movie, *Annie Hall.* Annie and Woody are both talking to their analysts, and there is a split screen.

Psychiatrist: *(To Annie)*
"How many times a week
do you make love?"

Annie:
"Constantly!
Four times a week!"

Psychiatrist: *(To Woody)*
"How many times a week do
do you make love?"

Woody:
"Hardly ever!
Four times a week."

Each of us reserves the right to have our own opinions and come to our own conclusions. How many times have we watched a stubborn child, or, even worse, an impossible teen-ager, make the same mistakes that we did, years ago? Have you ever tried to tell the young person that he or she is doing wrong? Doesn't work, does it?

How, then, can we expect that when we have differences with supposed "adults," who are even more crystallized in their thinking than young people, we are going to convince them that we know better than they what's in their "best interests?" The moment we convince ourselves we can impose our will upon another person, that's the moment we doom any type of constructive problem-solving to failure.

Remember our first rule: Every person wants to do what he or she perceives to be in his or her own best interests.

The moment Owner says to Builder, "I'm prepared to allow you to determine what's in your own best interests," and Builder responds, "I am prepared to allow *you* to determine what's in *your* own best interests," we have taken another giant step on the road to constructive, mutual problem resolution.

C) Now we come to the third basic rule: **Every person wants to keep as much power to himself or herself as possible, and every person wants to give away as little power as possible.**

That rule seems to be so clear and simple—how could anyone argue with it?

Yet in our current litigation-prone society, that is often the very first rule we break. The moment you walk into a lawyer's office and sign a retainer agreement, you immediately turn over responsibility for your fate to the lawyer. At the same time, you turn over a certain degree of decision-making power to the lawyer. Now the lawyer, not you, will dictate the procedural steps that may end up in arbitration or on the courthouse steps.

Take Art Owner, for example. As soon as he hired Barrister, he turned over money to Barrister. Barrister then thought that in order to justify the fees he charged, he ought to assume a role superior to that of Owner. It was now Barrister's recommendation to proceed through the court system. Owner handed over his ultimate power—the power to work out his own settlement with Builder—to Barrister. Builder, by going to Defensor, likewise handed over a similar degree of power.

The moment the lawyers and the clients decided to file a lawsuit, each party lost a little more power—the power to control the expenditure of money. That power became more eroded as time went on and the **lawyers** rather than the clients decided to hire experts, take depositions, and engage in various legal maneuvers. Ultimately, if the parties go to arbitration, court trial, or jury trial, each gives up the ultimate power—the power to make a final decision that governs his or her life with respect to this dispute.

Even at the last moment, when Owner and Builder ultimately took some degree of power back into their own hands, when they finally decided to settle the case—several thousands of dollars and many years later—the **lawyers** were directing how Owner and Builder would exercise that power and the **judge** had pretty well decided for them how it should be settled.

The minute you give power to lawyers, they interfere with your power to make a decision. When you and the party on the other side give power over to the judge or the jury, each of you totally gives away **all** your power to make a decision. A judge or a jury is a third person who neither knows you, cares about you, nor particularly wants to make an "objective" decision that will seriously impact your life. The judge or the members of the jury won't, in all likelihood, ever see you again and probably wouldn't recognize you if they did.

Conversely, the moment you decide constructively to resolve your dispute with another person, whatever that dispute may be, you keep all the decision-making power in your own hands. And if you never give it to the lawyer in the first place, you truly keep maximum power over your destiny from start to finish.

Although Owner and Builder have decided to negotiate rather than litigate, the "facts" as each party perceives them and the emotional involvement of the two parties may be such that while they might agree on minor points, when it gets down to basic issues, they may not be able to resolve their problem alone.

Enter the mediator.

Since lawyers have been schooled in logical problem-solving, since they come from a history, often forgotten, where they were counselors first, then advocates, there is no reason why lawyers cannot act as mediators—provided they, too, are willing to adjust their way of thinking and provided the public is able to change **their** way of thinking about lawyers.

To be an effective mediator requires not only problem-solving skills, but also:

1) The ability to listen actively to both sides;
2) The ability to maintain not only actual neutrality, but the appearance of neutrality;
3) A great deal of patience;
4) A very high tolerance for frustration; and
5) The desire and ability to keep a dialogue going in the midst of ballistic emotions.

At present, law schools are starting to give courses in mediation and alternative dispute resolution, but the bottom line when it comes to mediation is not book learning. Rather it is a certain mind-set, coupled with the human experience necessary to understand what makes people act the way they do. It is the ability to accept that a perfectly rational, mature man or woman may make what appears to be a disastrous choice and proceed to act on that choice because he or she perceives it to be in his or her best interests.

The mediator must not allow himself or herself to intrude on what a party feels to be his best interests, for then he or she violates a basic rule of mediation.

The ultimate purpose of true mediation differs completely from arbitration in the following basic way: The arbitrator will make a decision for the parties. In short, the *arbitrator* will dictate to them what their best interests are. The *mediator's* job, on the other hand, is to assist the *parties* in deciding upon a resolution that is in their own best interests.

The great historical novelist Gary Jennings probably best summed up my perception of the role of a mediator when, in his superb novel, *Raptor,* he attributed the following statement to Theodoric the Great, said to have been made in 500 A.D.:

> "I try to keep in mind one thing that all people should, but seldom do. It is that every person—king, commoner, slave—man,

woman, eunuch, child—every dog and cat, too, for all I know—
is the center of the universe. That fact ought to be self evident to
each of us. But we—being each the center of the universe—do
not often pause to realize that *so is everyone else.* A man may defer
to a god, or to several gods, to an overlord, to family elders, to any
number of acknowledged superiors. And I am not speaking of
self-love or self-importance. A man may love his children more
than himself. And he may never feel important at all. Very few
people ever have any legitimate reason for feeling important.

"Nevertheless, to any man's sight and hearing and understanding, every other thing in the universe revolves about him. How
could it seem otherwise? From inside his head, he regards everything else as outside, existing only insofar as it affects himself.
Thus his own interest must be paramount. What he believes is,
to him, the only necessary truth. What he does not know is not
worth knowing. What things he does not love or hate are, to him,
matters of no concern whatever. His own needs and wants and
complaints deserve the most immediate attention. His own
rheumatism is of more moment than another's dying of the car-
rion worm. His own impending death means the veritable end of
the world.

"Can any of you conceive of even the grass growing when
you can no longer feel it springy underfoot? When you can
no longer smell its sweet aroma after rain? When you can no
longer loose your faithful horse to graze upon it? When the grass
has no other reason for growing but to mantle your grave—and
you are not even able to admire that?'

"So, when any person requires my attention—senator, swine-
herd, prostitute—I try to remind myself: the grass grows, the
world exists, only because this person lives. His or her concerns
are the most pressing ever brought before me. And then, in
addressing those concerns, I try to bear in mind that the disposi-
tion I make of them will inexorably affect *other* centers of the
universe. Perhaps I make it sound either fatuously simplistic or
confoundingly tangled, but I believe my attempt at perspective
enables me to judge and pronounce and rule more providently.
Anyway, the people seem satisfied."

If all of us, disputants and mediators alike, bear this wisdom in mind, then mediation—indeed any problem-solving exercise—is bound to be successful. Once we change our attitude from, "How can I destroy that blankety-blank?" to "How can we achieve a win-win result for each of us?" we will more successfully be able to define the role of the attorney in our society.

CHAPTER 8

The Nuts and Bolts of Mediation

Corrupt Businessman's telegram to his lawyer:
"Please advise results of my case."
Lawyer's telegraphic response: "Justice has triumphed!"
Businessman's reply telegram: "Appeal Immediately!"

WNER AND BUILDER have resolved some of their problems by agreeing to negotiate. They are unable to come to complete agreement, except that they have agreed to mediate the remaining problems. How does mediation work?

First, the parties should select an impartial mediator, someone whom neither of them knows or has ever dealt with before. The reason for this is to avoid even the *appearance* of partiality. Should it be someone in the trades, an officer of a homeowner's association, a judge, a lawyer, or someone else?

The problem of selection is not as difficult as it sounds at first. Any individual with a reasonable amount of maturity, experience in dealing with problem resolution, and some idea of the parameters of the problem is an appropriate candidate. The need for a great deal of technical expertise is not essential, except in a situation where two experienced tradesmen, professionals, or members of a select and limited group have need for mediation on a matter requiring technical experience.

The parties must agree in advance that this is not going to be an exercise in presentation of evidence. They are not using mediation to prove something in the sense of going to a court of law.

One of the major differences between litigation and mediation is that in a court of law, the parties try to re-create the past. And since an event is perceived by a specific witness from a specific point of view, the court can never arrive at "the truth."

In mediation, on the other hand, each party starts at ground zero. History begins right now, not at some time in the past. Each party will tell the mediator—and the other party—what he or she feels to be the dispute *at that moment*. The parties and the mediator work forward from that point.

While there is no reason why the mediator cannot be an attorney or a judge, the important question is **should** the mediator be an attorney or judge? On the one hand, lawyers and jurists are schooled in advocacy and decision-making, rather than achieving results through mediation. On the other hand, American society has traditionally charged attorneys and judges with resolving its problems.

If the parties are considering a specific judge or lawyer, particularly one whom they don't know, they should obtain many qualified opinions as to the proposed mediator's intelligence, integrity, flexibility, and temperament as someone who basically loves people and wants to help them help themselves.

How is a mediation handled? Each party decides in advance that he or she is going to be responsible for his or her share of the mediator's fee. The parties should find out in advance how much the mediator will charge. Although I believe that management, control, and reduction of legal fees is essential, placing a cap on the mediator's fees creates unnecessary stress. A good mediator will know within the first hour or two whether or not the effort will bear fruit.

Mediation should be conducted in a place that is completely neutral, usually at the mediator's office. In the case of Owner and Builder, the parties may think they should view the building site with the mediator. While the old saying that "a picture is worth a thousand words" is appropriate in litigation, it is totally irrelevant in mediation, since it is a problem-solving rather than a finger-pointing experience. Remember, we are using **now** as the starting point.

One of the finest mediators I know uses the following statement when he first meets with the parties:

"I want you to know that I have never met either of you. Thus I have no preconceived ideas of what your dispute is all about. Believe it or not, it is not **that** important that I know the 'facts' of this case, because we're not here today to review evidence. The 'facts' are just a frame of reference, and they are different for anyone who views them from a vantage point of his or her own perspective.

"Our perceptions and our perspective can be greatly altered if we know how the other person perceives something. I remember mediating a marital dissolution where I asked one of the parties, point blank, why she was engaging in a certain activity. She responded, quite honestly, 'Because I am angry and I want to annoy him in any way I can.' I then asked the husband, 'Does your wife's activity in doing that annoy you? He responded, 'No.' From that point forward, the parties began to talk constructively, because the wife found that she had totally misperceived what bothered her husband.

"We have certain rules in this mediation. First, each of you wants to act in your own best interests. We are trying to define and meet your best interests as known to you. Your best interests, as defined by you, can be any number of things: To be happy; to teach someone a lesson; to be angry; to force someone out of town; to get as much power as you can; to get even; to get as much money as you can; to leave the other person with as little as possible; to hurt the other person as much as you can; even to love as much as you can.

"If you came here with a plan for the other person, or to define the other person's best interests for him or her, you are doomed to frustration. I have never seen anyone able to define anyone else's best interests. If your own best interest is not to be frustrated, you might want to consider giving up your plan for the other person's best interests and simply take care of yourself.

"There is only one procedural rule: One person talks at a time. That means please don't interrupt, or, conversely, stop talking when someone else starts."

That was the sum and substance of that mediator's introductory remarks. Everything flows from there. Although the mediator has laid down a single ground rule, it is amazing how, if that ground rule is obeyed, the parties start listening as well as talking. At first, each defensive, the parties will usually talk to **impress.** Sooner or later, they speak to **express.** When they do that, the lines of communication begin to open.

I have attended several mediations with this particular mediator. He takes a completely neutral stance on whether or not the parties' attorneys attend the mediation. When I asked him his preference, he told me, "Usually, if the situation is emotionally charged or if there is a great deal of fear among the participants, I find it helpful for the lawyers to attend. Each party feels less vulnerable, less threatened, when he or she has his or her attorney present. As a general rule, lawyers are not quite as emotionally tied to the situation as the clients. They know that ultimately, if the dispute isn't settled through mediation, someone, usually the court, will make the decision, whether through strong-arm tactics at the settlement conference or at the trial itself.

"So lawyers can act as catalysts to start the process going. If the lawyers are motivated by good will and the honest desire to see the parties reach a settlement, they can be a great deal of help in making the playing field even and in making the parties see that they have nothing to fear.

"Once the lawyers have put in their appearance, quite often the parties have no difficulty if they wait in the other room while I talk to the parties. Some lawyers feel very threatened by this. They are afraid they might lose a large fee, or that the position they assert on behalf of their client may somehow be compromised. But I feel that most lawyers really would prefer to avoid the expense and hassle of a trial, and that most attorneys really do have their client's best interests at heart; otherwise they would not have encouraged and motivated their clients to accept mediation in the first place."

A mediator's greatest gifts are patience, an unflappable attitude, diplomacy, tact, and the ability to bring the parties together in viewing mediation as **constructive** problem resolution. "We are a team, trying to work out the best strategy that will achieve a win-win situation for everyone concerned. That may not always be as difficult as it seems, once we clear away the debris of what we initially think our best interests may be."

A major part of the mediator's job is listening—God gave us two ears and one mouth so we can listen twice as much as we talk. A mediator's talent to convince the opposing party that it is in his or her best interests to listen and hear what the other side is saying is critical.

I have learned from my own experience as a mediator that there comes a point where, suddenly and without advance planning on anyone's part, things become clear and a settlement falls into place. Quite often, it is not what I, as mediator, thought it would be, planned it to be, or encouraged it to be. It is something the parties reach of their own accord—seemingly completely independent of the mediator.

That is the best and most gratifying kind of mediation, because it is true mediation in the most basic sense of the word: the mediator has created an **atmosphere** where the parties ultimately—and happily—come together and resolve their own problems.

A recent example of a successful mediation involved a case between two lawyers. Each was financially successful. Each had a smooth, well-running personal injury mill. Several years ago, one of these lawyers had worked for the other. The break-up of their association had been acrimonious. For nine years following the dissolution of their association, each had sued the other on numerous occasions; each had reported the other to the State Bar; each had testified as witness against the other. When I entered the picture, they were in the ninth incarnation of their litigation. This particular lawsuit involved a dispute over a paltry $1,500.

From the very beginning, the attorneys representing these lawyers told them that their dispute was insane, and that they would spend thousands of dollars on this case alone. It didn't matter. Money truly wasn't an object to these stubborn advocates. "Justice" was.

Ultimately, with the "collusion" of the attorneys for these lawyers, the presiding judge of our court ordered both parties to mediate their differences in good faith. The two lawyer-clients grudgingly went to the mediator and listened.

The atmosphere was as tense as I have ever seen in a courtroom. After the mediator's introductory remarks, the two attorneys for the lawyer-clients excused themselves.

An hour later, the mediator came to consult the two attorney-disputants. He looked haggard and frustrated and said, "I have left your clients in the same room for a few minutes, but I think this is impossible. I have always believed I could mediate anything to a successful resolution, but this defies anything I've ever tried. Please don't ask me ever to mediate between lawyers again."

After a brief cup of coffee, he returned to his office. He came out less than five minutes later and called us into his office. He said, "While I was talking with you, your two clients settled all of their differences." He was as stunned as we were, but the rewards were instant and, so far, they have been lasting.

The parties dismissed their actions against one another. A week later, I received a call from the other lawyer's attorney, who said, "It looks like we have another potential case. Your client took another client away from mine. Is there any way we can get them talking so that they can agree on a division of fees?"

I immediately telephoned my client and said, "Please call your former associate and try to resolve this with him **before** it gets out of hand."

The following day, I received another call from the other attorney, thanking me for my intervention. "The two lawyers got together and resolved the division of fees in less than five minutes. In fact, they're now talking about referring difficult clients to one another."

The moral of this story is: If two people as difficult and unyielding as two lawyers who have been sworn enemies for several years can resolve their differences through mediation, why can't we all? And in so doing, the parties might just find common ground to renew a favorable relationship in the future. One caveat: The mediator cannot and should not inject himself or herself into the picture or give personal opinions as to how the parties should resolve their differences. The moment the mediator does that, he or she violates one of the cardinal rules: no one except the involved party has the right to decide what is or is not in his or her best interests.

It may well be that initially one or both parties may feel that litigation truly is in his or her best interests, just as in its most simplistic terms, a physical fight is the simplest, most basic, and certainly most direct way to resolve differences.

I am reminded of one of the most direct and "civilized" ways I have ever seen a dispute settled. The president of a highly successful regional airline discovered that another company was using the same advertising slogan. As it happens, the two companies had devised the slogan completely independently of one another, but the slogan was such that only one company could use it to advantage.

The president of the airline called the president of the second company. "Look," he said. "We can each spend about a hundred thousand dollars or more on high-priced lawyers, and by that time the slogan won't be worth a damn to anybody. Tell you what—how tall are you?"

"About five-ten," the president of the second company responded.

"About the same as me. How old are you?"

"Fifty-one."

"I spot you a year or so there. How much do you weigh?"

"One seventy-five."

"Do you work out?"

"Tennis about twice a week. I walk some."

"How about this? We meet in Las Vegas ten days from now and have an arm-wrestling contest. Winner takes the slogan and the loser pays for dinner."

"Why not?" the other said. "OK, you've got yourself a deal."

For the next ten days, although neither said anything, the two CEOs worked out like crazy—in their offices, in the gym, after dinner. Each brought his wife to Las Vegas on the appointed day. I won't spoil the story by telling you who won—obviously one of them did, and they had a marvelous weekend together afterward.

Wouldn't it be nice if we could settle all our problems like that?

Returning to reality, and to mediation, it has been my experience that when a mediator acts as the **medium** through which positive energy flows to the parties, he or she provides the ultimate service: assisting the parties in realizing that at some point on the circle, their best interests join and coalesce.

Such a result raises problem resolution to the plane of spiritual involvement, and the realization that sometimes giving up a position is not only the most beneficial way to realize a party's best interests, but also the best way to promote those interests successfully.

In the next chapters, we will see how mediation can successfully be employed in virtually every situation in which we now resort to the time-cumbersome, cost-ineffective, emotion-destroying court-and-lawyer system.

CHAPTER 9

The End of the World—
Mediation in the
Context of Divorce

"In a thousand pounds of law, there's not an ounce of love."
— **English proverb**

"Judges, as a class, display, in the matter of arranging alimony,
that reckless generosity which is found only in men who are
giving away someone else's cash."
— **P.G. Wodehouse**

STATISTICALLY ONE OUT OF EVERY THREE American marriages ends in divorce. The breakdown of a marriage is an emotionally wrenching process for the divorcing couple, their children, their relatives, and their friends. It is made far worse by today's divorce proceedings, which are needlessly intrusive, lengthy, expensive, and hostile, and which create an atmosphere so poisonous that it makes it difficult to cooperate in the future to raise children, dispose of marital assets, or do anything except hate. That compounds the tragedy many times over and perpetuates ill will into the next generation. What a travesty on justice.

I recently became involved in one of the most bizarre domestic situations in all my years of practice. I share it with you only to show how the legal system has completely broken down.

Mr. G is 87 years old. Mrs. G is 76. They married twenty-three years ago—the second marriage for each. They had been together for twenty years before that. Mr. G has two daughters from a previous marriage. Mrs. G has one daughter, also from a previous marriage. Mr. G receives a small pension, plus his Social Security and Medicare each month. Mrs. G also receives Social Security. They bought a home in Carmel, California. Six years ago, Mr. G was diagnosed as suffering from intermittent Alzheimer's disease, senile dementia, and progressive cancer.

Four years ago, Mrs. G found that she could not care for her husband alone. She placed him in a convalescent home with 24-hour skilled nursing care. His daughters objected, so Mrs. G brought him back home. But she was totally unable to care for him. Things got so bad that he was lying in his own excrement. Mrs. G placed him back in the convalescent home again. Since she did not want interference from his daughters, she did not tell them where he was.

Mr. G, fearing that the convalescent home was a permanent arrangement, told the attendants that if they did not call his daughters to fetch him, he would simply walk out. The daughters came, removed him, and took him to live with one of them.

Mrs. G and the daughters refused to work with one another. The daughters had their father in their home, but Mrs. G held the family's purse strings and refused to send any but minimal amounts to the daughters for her husband's care. She maintained that he had a perfectly good home with her, and there was no need for him to live with his daughters and have them spend unnecessary sums on nursing care.

Mr. G became ever more fearful (whether through the intercession of the daughters or simply from his own experience) that if he went back to live with his wife, he would end up in a convalescent home again.

The lines were now drawn deep in the sand. Instead of sitting down and mediating the situation—which both parties later said they wanted to do, but which neither formally suggested to the other—the daughters petitioned the court to be appointed conservators of their father's estate. That meant a court-ordered turnover of some of his funds to the daughters to enable them to provide care for him without constantly begging their stepmother for money.

Mrs. G felt she did not have the finances or the knowledge properly to fight the motion, which was filed in a court 75 miles away from her home. She could not afford to have the four doctors who had diagnosed her husband take a day from their practices to travel to and from the court—at a cost of $2,500 apiece. On the strength of their father's expressed desire, the daughters obtained the conservatorship.

Mrs. G retained a new lawyer, who said that her prior lawyer, who had charged her $10,000, had not done a good job. Under the second lawyer's direction, she appealed the court's ruling in the conservatorship proceedings.

Now the stakes were dramatically raised. Telephone calls between Mr. and Mrs. G became hostile. Mr. G felt his wife was holding onto **his** money, that she no longer loved him, and that the only reason she was holding onto the money was so he would have to come home and she could put him in a convalescent home. Mrs. G denied that, and claimed Mr. G was wholly under the influence and control of his daughters. Mr. G threatened to file divorce proceedings unless Mrs. G turned over what he felt to be **his** money. She refused.

Thereafter, with Mr. G's blessing, the daughters filed divorce proceedings on his behalf. Mrs. G hired a third attorney in the distant city. Instead of promptly moving for an order to transfer the case to Mrs. G's county, the lawyer filed her response in the same court as had originally heard the conservatorship proceedings, nominally because Mr. G now lived in that jurisdiction, but actually because it was more convenient for him to go to that court because his office was in that city.

Within two months of their being retained, the divorce lawyers petitioned the court to allow **each** of them to take a $15,000 advance as a nonrefundable retainer fee. The **lawyers** then signed a stipulation that the court could grant such an order. Since the matter was "uncontested," the court granted the fee request. Then the daughters' lawyer petitioned the court to allow them a fee of

$14,000 from the marital property to pay for **them** obtaining the conservatorship.

By the time I became involved in the case, more than $50,000 had been spent on attorneys' fees. The vast majority of that money was needlessly squandered by parties who could ill afford it, simply because no one had the common sense to control Mr. G, Mrs. G and the daughters, and tell them at the very beginning that what they were doing would effectively part them from more than a third of all their property.

This case is, perhaps, the most flagrant example of the system breaking down and, so far as I am concerned, **stealing** what those two old people had saved with which to live out their lives.

Except in a very few cases, marital separation does not come suddenly or without warning. In no event does it come easily. The words "'til death do us part," and "What God hath joined, let no man put asunder," carry a great deal of moral and persuasive force, as well they should, especially when children are involved. Even without the exacerbation of the court system, divorce leaves its scars for a lifetime: guilt, anger, embarrassment, the crying of men, women, and children in the night, the thought that those involved are somehow losers because they weren't able to keep their marriage intact.

But divorce does occur. There are almost no families left in the United States that have not experienced it among their number.

Historically, divorce proceedings were preoccupied with "fault." To this day, many lawyers and judges in New York remember when adultery was the primary ground for divorce and, after divorcing couples had worked out the property division and alimony arrangements, all that remained was to hire a model to pose, half-naked, in the bed of the "guilty" spouse, while "incriminating" photographs were taken. Today we laugh at what seems a quaint morality play from another era. But a shrinking number of states still require that one spouse prove "grounds" for divorce. That means a spouse must testify in court about some act of "mental cruelty," or some other legally acceptable ground. The charade not only encourages perjury, it makes a mockery of the court process.

Even though most states provide for "no fault" divorce, with no grounds required except "incompatibility" or "incurable insanity," getting a divorce today is still needlessly cruel and complicated. Couples who are already anxious and vulnerable receive all sorts of frightening misinformation and hear horror stories from well-meaning friends and family members. The overwhelming scare tactic employed over the years reflects the basic fears of each side:

Husband: I'm going to take the children from her. Or if she gets custody, I'll make sure she doesn't get a dime in support.

Wife: I'm going to take the blankety-blank for every penny he's got. He'll be so poor he won't be able to pay attention; and I'll get an alimony order that'll crush him.

As time goes on, both husband and wife learn that neither can accomplish their threats. By then, lawyers' fees and expert witness fees have soaked up a hefty percentage of these assets the husband and wife worked so long to accrue.

There's got to be a better way.

Divorce should be taken out of the court system entirely. We should do away with the false "grounds." We should devise a system that will preserve whatever dignity and self-esteem the couple have left, so that neither is afraid to enter into another, hopefully more lasting relationship if such be their inclination.

I propose what I'll call the "long building concept," in which a couple contemplating marital dissolution would go through several "offices," administered impartially by state agencies, with no lawyers involved. At the end of their time in the building, they would be entitled to a decree dissolving their marriage. Any couple desiring to divorce would enter the building and first go through pre-dissolution counseling, either one-on-one or in the context of a small seminar session involving similarly situated couples. The seminar would cover the following areas of concern:

1) Are there alternatives to what we think we want to do?
2) What will the personal and emotional effects be on each of us?

3) How do we handle interpersonal relationships and communications with our divorcing spouses, in-laws, etc., before, during and after divorce?
4) How do we break this news to the children, relatives and friends?
5) What can we realistically expect from society? This would cover a wide range of subjects ranging from church condemnation to the perils of dating after many years as a married person.
6) What can we realistically expect in regard to child custody, child support, spousal support and the like?
7) What can we realistically expect regarding the division of property and our own financial condition after the divorce?
8) What are the best ways to "float away" from one another rather than destroy each other?

As the anxiety quotient diminishes, many couples may find that for the first time in years they are able to work together. This type of pre-divorce counseling might even result in some couples, who felt they had nothing in common, staying together.

The initial seminar would be a broad, nonspecific overview, and, with input from other couples contemplating divorce, the parties could obtain comfort from the feeling, "We're not alone. We're not the only ones going through this process." Although it seems unfair to compare the seminar with a childbirth class, the similarities are probably greater than the differences. At the end of the seminar session, there could be a brief, oral, non-threatening "exam" that would reinforce what the couple had learned, and would re-emphasize the importance of a constructive attitude toward the divorce.

The next series of offices in the "long building" would be emotional counselors. The couple would attend counseling sessions to inquire into the underlying basis for the divorce and try to explore the reasons for the problems. Virtually every counselor—indeed most lawyers—know that the reasons for divorce are generally limited to:

1. **Sexual difficulties.** This is by far the greatest problem in all age groups. A psychologist once told me, "When sex is good, that takes care of about 80 percent of the problems in marriage. But when sex is no good, the husband and wife have a lot of explaining to do—mostly to themselves." I need not go into the range of problems, which include everything from unfaithfulness to impotence to frigidity, but since this is the most intimate part of the most intimate relationship known to human beings, it would seem fairly obvious that this is a "marriage breaker." Yet I am surprised at how many divorcing couples play the game of giving every other reason imaginable—"We just don't communicate" is the most common—for the marital breakdown.

2. **Children.** Although many couples still subscribe to the admonition to "stay together for the children's sake," children themselves often unknowingly contribute to marital difficulties. That can run the gamut from the husband being jealous because his wife, who is now primarily a mother, doesn't give him the time or attention she used to, to differences in how to raise the children ("You spoil them rotten!" "You just don't understand. Our children have so much less than their classmates!"), to reactions when the children become teenagers and do or say things that adversely reflect on their parents. Unquestionably, when a child enters the family unit, it becomes a different unit than it was when the couple first got married.

A reversal of that situation occurs in mature marriages, when the children are grown and gone. All too often, the couple has devoted their lives to the children. In the process, they have forgotten how important it is to communicate with one another. Once the children are out of the house, the house seems empty, and the couple has no shared interests, conversation, or sense of intimacy left.

3. **In-law problems.** Although this has its most dramatic effect on younger couples, bitterness may poison the marriage from start to finish. In most—but by no means all—

cases, it is mother-in-law versus daughter-in-law. A man never ceases being a little boy at heart—a secret every woman knows. As such, he feels beholden to his mother. Now he is placed between the proverbial rock and a hard place. What is he supposed to do? Where do his loyalties lie? All too often, whatever choice he makes, it's the wrong one.

4. **Money problems.** This problem is more prevalent in the United States than elsewhere. We are a capitalistic society. Television and the media exhort us every day to buy, buy, buy. Ultimately, our profligate spending catches up with us. What happens when we can no longer afford to buy the expensive toys that spouse or children demand as social "necessity?" What happens when the breadwinner loses his job? Or takes to drinking? Or simply becomes burned out?

5. **Communication problems.** This is a big catch-all, and perhaps not a realistic one. It is simply a failure to deal with the other four problems in a timely, adult manner. The old saying, "You grow together or you grow apart," is true. Marriage, like any other relationship, is a dynamic thing: it moves forward or backward, but it never remains static.

In order for mediation to be successful in the context of divorce, the "long building" must be equipped to deal with the four major problems: sex, children, in-laws and money. By so doing, it would be designed to resolve the problem of communication, even if the parties' own best interests (remember that term from the last chapter?) decree that they become divorced.

Both men and women become most sensitive when anything having to do with sex is discussed. Perhaps the "long building" should have an office devoted to sexual counseling as an optional form of mediation. In any event, professionals must deal with emotional counseling. Many large corporations have adopted the practice of "out-placement counseling." The type of counseling I envision here is similar. People are about to leave a relationship and a status—marriage—and enter into a situation where they are alone once again—whether voluntarily or involuntarily.

That will mean personal adjustments. The more information a man or woman going through divorce has to help him or her deal with the situation, the less fearful he or she will be and the less stressful the divorce. The group concept is a non-threatening means of letting the couple know that they are not alone in marital dissolution.

The next office in the "long building" would be devoted to family and child counseling. Regardless of how many marital breakups there are today, regardless of how cold and barren a couple's marriage may be, a child's greatest fear is that mommy and daddy will divorce.

While children may intellectualize that it is the best thing for their parents, it is far and away the worst thing for **them.** They must adjust to new allegiances and to choices they don't want to make.

Divorcing husbands and wives often seek alliances with the children. The children are then placed in the position of "choosing." The underlying implication throughout—never said out loud—is, "If you love your father, you obviously love me less, because you should know what a rotten person he is." Such an attitude results in the children "taking sides," but they do so falsely. Children are tough survivors. They know that if they are going to survive the holocaust in their lives, they **must** play one parent against the other. That usually results in telling one parent what he or she wants to hear about the other and taking back false messages or mixed messages to the other.

Parents don't realize that every time they encourage such partisanships, every time they allow the child to know how good it feels that the child is taking his or her side in a dispute, they are only creating deep desperation and unhappiness in the child. That type of instant gratification for the "innocent" parent will almost certainly come back to haunt that parent later in life, when the now-adolescent child turns on the "good guy" parent and blames that parent for irretrievably ruining the relationship the child might have had with the other parent. This type of partisan-solicitation will also serve to make the child suspicious and unwilling to enter into a meaningful, open, intimate relationship later.

Children fear—rightly—that their daily lives will be shattered. Whether or not their friends view them as pariahs, or worse, as objects of pity, children **perceive** they are being so viewed. And they will react, generally, by taking on new friends—invariably more aggressive, daring children (often other victims of divorce) who will provide the "company" in the term "misery loves company."

Children fear they will be physically displaced, that they will have to move from their neighborhood, go to a new school, make a whole new series of friends, and, even worse, have to leave their newly found associates every week "to go visit dad" (or mom, since joint custody or the father as primary custodial parent have gained momentum).

Children also have even deeper emotional scars: they feel they are to blame for the divorce. If they had been "good" little boys and girls, it would not have happened. They try everything possible to get daddy and mommy back together.

Fear often displays itself in the form of anger, particularly where there is a replacement of mom or dad by a new social interest of the opposite, or even the same, sex. Children feel that any new union is both unnatural and wrong. Often they will lash out either at the parent who has a new romantic interest, or at the person who has supplanted the divorcing parent.

Thus it is necessary to consider the children's needs in the divorce and bring them into the equation in order to defuse the worst fear of all: fear of the unknown.

Many times, one party does everything possible to frustrate visitation. When a child becomes conveniently "sick" on visitation day, the custodial parent immediately becomes more sympathetic with the child's "illness" than ever before. Or the custodial parent may become "sick" and ask the child to stay home to care for mommy or daddy. Those who have found themselves in child custody and visitation "games" will find this scenario all too familiar.

Invariably when one parent or the other has contacted me with great fears about the other parent "stealing" or running off with the child, and wants me to obtain a restraining order limiting visitation to the minimum the law allows, my comment is: "Is that

really in your best interests? Cool down a little. Think about whether or not it would be in your own best interests to let [the other parent] have the child for as long as he or she wants."

A fearful mother argues: How could it **possibly** be in her best interests (or, to use the more critical "buzz word"—how could it be in the **child's** best interests) to let this poor, innocent child, "who is only five years old" be alone with her father, who has never taken care of her and wouldn't know how?

The answer is simple. Part of the mystique of the father demanding the child is his fear that the mother will do everything in her power to remove him as an influential force in the child's life. The father reacts in the only way he can: with force and threats to take the child away—perhaps permanently. Although such a threat is, for the most part, empty, it certainly frightens the mother into heavy-duty retaliatory action.

Consider the mediated alternative. Assume that the mother says to her divorcing spouse, "Not only do I want you to have as much time as possible with our child, but I insist you have the child with you at least half the time—starting today."

Would that defuse the situation? And how! It doesn't take dad long to find out that he isn't going to be a "Disneyland daddy" (the kind who takes the child to the amusement park on his weekend visitations because he doesn't know what else to do). Now that he has the child with him half of every week, he's going to have some wonderful new experiences. He'll have to:

1) Learn to cook and do dishes (taking the child out for dinner every night quickly gets tiresome and expensive);
2) Put up with the child's increasing obnoxiousness as weariness sets in;
3) Help the child with homework;
4) Make sure the child gets to bed at a decent hour;
5) Make sure the child gets to school on time the next morning;
6) Make sure the child has a lunch packed and ready to go;
7) Learn to live with a restricted lifestyle that the mother has lived with for years.

There's an old saying: "Be careful what you wish for; you may get it." After a week, dear old dad will think long and hard about his threat to take the child away permanently.

From mom's point of view, she has to face certain things by giving the child up three nights a week to her divorcing husband:

1) She has practically no dishes to wash and no responsibility for the time the child is with its father;
2) She has freedom to do adult things she's missed out on for years, whether that be a women's support group, a night class at college, or a date;
3) She finds that the limited amount of money available for child support or spousal support goes further because there's less need to buy so many clothes, so much junk food, and the other things that were necessary armaments in the "war" to secure the child's affection.

The antidote to fear is knowledge and candor.

Under the "long building" concept, the child, the parents, and the family counselor deal with everyday problems that they face in the divorce situation. Once the child learns that his or her parents cooperate in keeping communications open, he or she has less inclination (and certainly less power) to manipulate, because the parents know when the child is trying to take advantage of the situation. And the fewer court hassles there are over custody and visitation, the less the lawyers are paid. In fact, there is probably no need for lawyers at all.

Once the couple works the first hurdles out, the only major areas left are division of the marital assets and liabilities, child support, and spousal support.

In these days of two-wage families, the historic division of "the wife gets the house, the husband gets the business" may not always work. If the wife or husband is a doctor or lawyer, for example, it is unrealistic to award the other spouse the practice, particularly since that spouse is not legally qualified to engage in that profession.

Certain assets are easy to value and divide. A house has a reasonable, ascertainable fair market value. The "garage sale" value of expensive, one-of-a kind furniture is about 10 percent of what you paid for it. Retirement plans are such that actuaries can determine to the penny the value one spouse or the other has invested.

Historically, the difficulties have come in valuing a business or a professional practice, particularly where one spouse has been the "rainmaker"—the one who brings in the lion's share of the business and income—in his or her business or profession. If you remove the rainmaker, the business has **no** value. Additional difficulties come about when a husband or wife owned property **before** the marriage, and the couple have made improvements that have resulted in increased value.

In such circumstances, the standard practice has been that each side hires a valuation expert. (Remember Owner vs. Builder?) A lot of money that's needed for more important purposes can go out the door. Rather than fight over the values, which will be inconclusive at best, the "long building" would provide state-appointed, state-paid, independent appraisers in a number of fields. Rather than have the experts haggle needlessly over value, the appraiser would meet with the couple and discuss all aspects of the business, profession, or property.

Most states value the business or profession as of either the date of separation or the date of the divorce decree. Often, that is an unrealistic value. Suppose the wife, an artist, is negotiating for a one-woman show. The success of her show may be in doubt and she may wish to have valuation made right now because of the separation. On the other hand, the husband may feel that since she created the artworks during the marriage, he should share in the bounty should the show be successful.

The job of the appraiser-mediator would be to assist the husband and wife in agreeing on the appropriate value of the business, profession, etc., by pointing out ranges of value and matters which they should take into consideration. While the appraiser might retain the ultimate jurisdiction to make a decision should the parties not agree, the mediation process is meant to enable the parties to recognize that they serve their own best interests most positively when they enter into an educated agreement between themselves, a win-win situation with a minimum of bitterness.

That practice can extend into all aspects of valuation, including putting a dollar figure on the marital contribution to one spouse's separate property. Despite the current system of adversarial experts and litigation, most couples have a pretty good idea of the "ballpark" value of their assets. If placed in a **constructive** resolution mode, they are most likely to "horse trade" with one another until each is ultimately satisfied with the result.

The next aspect of marital dissolution can be sticky, but it doesn't have to be. In many states there now exist computer-assisted formulas for alimony and child support. Where once we played a guessing game, today's divorce lawyers use a hand-held computer with a "dissomaster" program that allows us to determine, within 10 percent either way, exactly what one spouse may expect to pay and the other may expect to receive. However, when you have two lawyers, each with a computer plugged in, there is still an element of chance. Like the "chancellor's arm" of yore, each side plugs different numbers and sets of circumstances into the computer and, surprise, the computers come up with different numbers.

Additionally, each party pays his or her lawyer the ".2" or whatever time it takes to play out the computer figures. And, as we demonstrated earlier, it may take less than two minutes to punch the appropriate keys, but by the time the lawyer "has done the work and gotten back to where he was when he started to punch the keys," two-tenths of an hour have gone by.

Another problem invariably rears its ugly head: whether considering child or spousal support, one party invariably inflates his or her needs artificially and the other manages to have virtually no disposable income. While the court always "reserves jurisdiction" to modify a spousal or child support award, getting into court to do that is contentious, expensive, and generates unnecessary lawyers' fees.

A final problem in this situation is that the concept of permanent spousal support—alimony—is, in many states, a thing of the past. The supported spouse often has to face the harsh reality that he or she will need to be retrained relatively quickly to make an income. The duration of spousal support has, over the years, become a thorny issue. The supported spouse often delays the retraining procedure, while the paying spouse equally often becomes impatient enough to go back to court to shorten the duration.

I propose that a financial adviser-mediator meet with the couple over a protracted period of time to help them set up their own time and payment schedule. Most important, this adviser should explain options and assist the parties in achieving their own best interests. Among the things the mediator-financial adviser can and should discuss with the parties are:

1) The income tax aspects of support. The supporting party can now take every dime of spousal support as a tax deduction and the supported party must declare such support as income. A recent development in law has been the concept of "family support" in lieu of child support or spousal support, which has tax benefits for both spouses.

2) Managing to live within the new financial parameters. There are numerous ways to make declining dollars stretch farther. Some of them include pumping your own gasoline at the gas station, shopping at discount stores, perhaps even considering spending $2,000 to put a remanufactured engine in the family car instead of $15,000 on a new one. The financial adviser should encourage the parties to be creative—and actually help them live within the new boundaries.

3) Managing retraining time creatively. The parties may set up a timetable for the supported party's vocational rehabilitation. If the supported party achieves financial independence faster than projected, he or she would receive a bonus from the supporting party.

4) Setting up spousal support so it would survive remarriage or another relationship. Under present law, a wife may prefer to refrain from remarrying or from publicly letting the world know she's living with another man, because of the sword of spousal support cutoff hanging over her head. It would be better, and certainly more honest, to set realistic, time-limited spousal support orders.

Court-ordered child support payments generally cease when the child attains majority (18), dies, or marries. This practice encourages either acrimony or begging, since the partner in the superior economic condition uses the threat of child support cutoff as a club. In the "long building," the parties would discuss alternatives, such as sharing college education expenses proportionate to their then-incomes, guaranteeing student loans for their children, or even extending low-cost loans to children who choose not to attend college, so they can get a head start in life.

When parties discuss constructive problem resolution in a non-threatening manner, without lawyers, without hostility, without court intercession, everyone profits.

One significant point that should occur in divorce is a continuing commitment to re-examination and flexibility. Needs do change. Earning abilities change. Values change. And circumstances change.

The parties should agree that:

1) For the first year after the divorce decree, they will return to a specified mediator once each quarter for a post-divorce checkup on how things are working out.

2) If either of them feels there is a need to proceed back to another mediator, they will both go back to any specific mediator whose needs are required (usually the financial planning mediator or the personal counseling mediator) for additional discussion and exploration of problems that may have arisen.

Finally, the parties proceed to the last office in the "long building"—an administrator who grants a certificate of marital dissolution, effective that day. The administrator need not be a highly skilled, highly paid, overworked judge. Rather, it could be a clerical person who would not need to exercise judicial discretion.

Wouldn't the whole procedure be far more expensive for the state—what with all the mediators and experts? Absolutely not. The parties would pay for the services they receive. Their payments would be substantially less than if the two of them paid attorneys and experts to engage in an adversarial divorce. The savings to the judicial system would be immense and judges could be freed from the antagonistic drudgery of divorces.

Through societal training, the parties would change their way of thinking from an "end of the world" mentality to one of: "This may not be the best thing that ever happened to me, but at least I don't have to fear for my future." The savings in emotional well-being, avoidance of permanent scarring of innocent children and vastly diminished lawyers' fees would be more than enough, whatever the cost.

And by changing the way we think, we could once again help foment the revolution to deliver justice more economically, more expeditiously, more cost-effectively, and more fairly in our society.

Mediation in a
Contract Dispute

If law school is so hard to get through,
how come there are so many lawyers?

– Calvin Trillin

There was a young lawyer who showed up at a revival meeting
and was asked to deliver a prayer. Unprepared, he gave a prayer
straight from the lawyer's heart:
"Stir up much strife amongst the people, Lord,"
he prayed, "lest thy servant perish."

– Senator Sam Ervin

THE DISPUTE BETWEEN Owner and Builder was a contract dispute. In Chapter 7, we opened the door to mediation. In Chapter 8, we demonstrated the mechanics of how mediation works. Owner and Builder might never do business with one another again. On the other hand, they might find a means of doing expanded business with one another as a creative alternative to litigation.

Suppose Owner owns a computer store. He can obtain equipment wholesale. Builder has wanted a computer network for his business for years, but has not had the available cash. Deep down, Builder may feel embarrassed for the screw-up on Owner's home, although he'd never admit it. If he could somehow turn the fiasco into a situation that might actually result in more business for him, he could make additional allowances for the completion of Owner's house. Owner has been having slow times in his computer store. By working constructively and creatively with the mediator, Owner and Builder might arrive at a dynamic resolution that far exceeds the initial expectations of either of them.

1) Owner does not have the $25,000 that Builder wants to finish the house. He does not want to borrow additional cash to pay Builder.

2) Owner and Builder arrive at a fair value settlement of $10,000 for Builder to complete the house. The actual cost to Builder to finish the house will be about $3,500 (remember, in Chapter 7, Builder thought he could do some of the work himself and make deals with some of the subcontractors). Owner and Builder agree that the house will be completed within thirty days.

3) Instead of paying cash, Owner agrees to install a computer network system for Builder at the best price Builder can find for that computer system at any other store or dealer. After shopping around, Owner and Builder agree on $15,000 as the price of the system that Builder wants. Since Owner will do much of the installation himself, the actual cost to Owner is $5,000.

4) Builder does not have $5,000 in cash. He does not want to borrow it if he doesn't have to. Owner needs some shelving, display work, and painting to spruce up his store. The parties agree on $5,000 worth of work.

5) Finally, the parties agree that if there is any problem, they will return to the mediator to help them resolve it. They make a commitment that they will not go to arbitration or to court, particularly since they have reached a win-win result for them both.

Does this resolution sound improbable or simplistic? It isn't. All one needs to remember is that in our free enterprise system, everyone has something that someone else needs. Our entire system is based on trade—the exchange of resources. If Owner is a lawyer, attorney's fees can be traded; if he owns a market, he can arrange through his suppliers to get a special deal for Builder on a side of beef. The possibilities are limited only by our imaginations.

Throughout this book, we have emphasized that we need to modify our idea of how best to dispense justice if we are to change the legal system. In virtually every situation, there comes a point when the best interests of each party join, if the parties search hard enough. The closest analogy I can think of is a statement I heard years ago when I visited the Griffith Planetarium in Los Angeles: Often, when we look for something by staring directly at where it's supposed to be, we miss it. But if we look out of the corner of our eye, we often sight the object we've missed. Let's expand the Owner versus Builder situation to a more complex arena of trade.

Farmer, acting through Broker, sells his entire year's crop of garlic to Wholesaler on a sliding scale, varying from 30 cents per pound for giant, first-grade cloves to 8 cents per pound for irregular ones. Wholesaler, acting through **his** Broker, sells the crop to the Supermarket chain for 45 cents per pound for giant cloves and 12 cents per pound for irregular ones, to be picked up at Farmer's field.

Three months into the growing season, half of Farmer's crop is destroyed. Farmer files for bankruptcy protection. The trustee in bankruptcy takes over the operation of the farm. Meanwhile, the Supermarket chain finds that its needs are greater than originally contemplated. Rancher, a new supplier, agrees to sell the Supermarket chain his entire crop for 42 cents per pound for giant cloves and 10 cents per pound for irregular ones. The Supermarket chain cancels its order from trustee in bankruptcy (who has taken over Farmer's position). The Trustee, the Wholesaler and the two Brokers all threaten to sue the Supermarket chain for breach of contract. In the midst of the threats, Rancher advises the Supermarket chain that he misquoted the price to the Supermarket chain due to a serious error made by his Accountant. The true price will be **46** cents per pound for giant cloves and **14** cents per pound for irregular ones. The Supermarket chain now threatens to sue Rancher for specific performance and Rancher threatens to sue his accountant.

It is now one month before the garlic is ready for harvest.

Problem No. 1: You are a lawyer acting under our present adversarial court system. One of the parties (pick any one you want), comes to you with the above statement of facts. How many parties can you sue? For what? How long will it take? How much do you think your fee will be?

Problem No. 2: You are one of the parties (pick any one you want to be). You agree with all the other parties that you'll try to work the problem out without going to the courts or the lawyers. List in their order of importance the things you define as being in your own best interests (including saving attorneys' fees).

Problem No. 3: All of the parties have agreed to go to mediation rather than spend hundreds of thousands of dollars on lawyers and court fees. They do not want an "expert" in the field, because they all know the position they're in. They all agree that you will make the perfect mediator due to your maturity and your fair attitude toward everyone concerned. You listen to the claims of each participant. Realizing that the parties are not expecting you to make their decision for them, but want you to assist them in resolving their dispute by recommending options and alternatives, what recommendations can you make?

Do you think this exercise is merely a silly game with no point to it? Actually, it's much more practical than you might think.

Being involved in a problem means knowing what the problem is all about: knowing the nature of the problem and the solution that you initially feel might be in your own best interests. In that regard, when you find yourself involved, you are part of the problem.

Becoming part of the solution is more complex, because it involves the unconscious. You can rely just so much on your five senses; after that, you must use your curiosity, imagination, and your capacity for skepticism—which is not to be confused with cynicism. Skepticism obliges you to look beneath the obvious to get at the true meaning of the situation.

True problem resolution compels you to think in new ways, to come up with fresh, previously untried solutions, to move beyond the obvious to the infinite. If you dare the absurd, sometimes you can achieve the impossible.

Here's a constructive exercise: Why not try in the context of your family or your co-workers to create problems—the more complex and "impossible" the better. Then try just as creatively to resolve them. Invariably you will find there are differences of opinion on how best to resolve them. There will always be more than one "right" answer, even if it turns out to be "the right answer to a different question."

You'll be surprised to find out how quickly you develop a sense of accomplishment in the successful resolution of theoretical conflicts. More important, it will demonstrate how easy it is to change the way you think in terms of conflict management.

And since changing the way we believe justice can—and should—be delivered is one thing on which we all can agree, we are starting with our goal already in sight.

CHAPTER 11

Managing Conflict
in the Workplace

Q. How many lawyers does it take to change a lightbulb?
A. How many can you afford?

THUS FAR, WE HAVE EXPLORED mediation in the context of several fields of human conflict. However, we have waited until now to explore that area where each of us rubs up against inherent conflict—actual or potential— every day of our lives: the workplace.

In 1964, our society started passing a series of laws designed to eliminate discrimination on the basis of sex, age, race, etc. As we have progressed down the road to "equality," we've passed more laws, and the courts have circumscribed more and more what we can say or do in the workplace. It used to be that when an employer hired an employee, it was "at will." Many state statutes still tell us this is the case. But an ever-growing number of lawsuits for "wrongful termination" speak more eloquently than statutes and ordinances, particularly when there have been some rather dramatic damage awards. The pendulum has recently swung back the other way, particularly in states such as California, where "wrongful termination" and "hostile workplace" lawsuits had reached epidemic proportions.

The problem is one of almost impossible complexity, but it can be simplified by recognizing a certain very painful reality of life today: Because of a combination of technology, overpopulation, and the need for our country to compete—and compete hard—in the global economy, there are simply too many people to fill the professionally and socially acceptable jobs.

The older worker claims seniority and refuses to be "pushed out the door" before he or she is good and ready. The younger, entry-level person, often a college graduate, is reduced to working as a waiter or at some other "menial" job because there are no job openings in his or her professed specialty. And the universities, in order to justify their existence and their increasingly high payrolls and tuition fees, must churn out new graduates every year.

That's a frightening reality—much more frightening than the specter of lawyers.

Such a situation is bound to produce stresses that were never there before. Union membership is slipping, and unions find themselves negotiating for job security rather than huge pay raises. Faced with increasingly stiff competition, and "downsizing" or "right-sizing" brought on by almost daily mergers and acquisitions, which result in that many fewer jobs, we have truly become a society where the "best and brightest," "the hard **and** smart workers," who are willing to take less and work longer hours, and those who have the strongest connections, are the only ones who survive.

Although the rules still allow time for talk, breaks, and official 9-to-5 hours, woe be to the employee who tries to enforce each and every one of those so-called rules to the letter. Such workers will find themselves "outplaced," another current buzz-word, very quickly.

Today, almost every written employment contract or employee manual stresses that the employee is an "at will" employee, meaning he or she can quit or be fired at will and with virtually no notice, for any reason. Additionally, the employment manuals emphasize that each employee agrees to arbitration of every one of his or her workplace disputes, including termination, thus waiving what had, in the past, been one of the employee's strongest weapons against the employer: the right to trial before a sympathetic jury.

While courts and legislatures seem to change the ground rules each year, all of us are now threatened with the realization that as technology progresses, the need for labor-intensive employment is diminishing. Not a week goes by that the media doesn't tell us that one major company or another is downsizing by eliminating a third of its jobs, that two large banks have merged with one another, or that a major airline company has filed for bankruptcy protection and, as part of its reorganization plan, is disaffirming its current union contracts.

The workplace, once a refuge from the stresses of domestic life, has become a place where the atmosphere is charged with tension and a defensive atmosphere. Management is afraid to fire a marginal worker, or test for drugs in the workplace, or even try to adjust hours and pay scales to save the company, for a lawsuit of some kind always looms on the horizon.

Labor worries because of its loss of bargaining position in the marketplace. Every car that comes in from Japan, every computer that comes in from Taiwan, every television set that comes in from Malaysia means there will be one less job in the United States. Although the North American Free Trade Agreement has been hailed as a panacea for American labor, American labor remains unconvinced and, if anything, NAFTA sets up a defensive role for the American laborer against the very party that labor has always supported.

Is there room for mediation in the employment arena? Or is that area of the law over-regulated already? The answer to these questions is neither clear-cut nor easy.

Yet the concept of mediation actually started in the labor arena. The federal government is empowered to "freeze" strikes and lockouts and bring the parties to a bargaining table presided over by a federal mediator. If an employee is a member of a union and party to a collective bargaining agreement (a union contract), his or her rights are generally represented by a shop steward or union attorney at no cost (except the ever-escalating union dues) to the employee.

But that does not always apply to cases of termination, particularly when the employer believes that the termination is for good cause and the employee believes the termination is wrongful, or constitutes a breach of the implied contract that he or she would not be fired except for good cause.

In the 1980s wrongful termination was the darling of plaintiffs' lawsuits, and a guarantee of plentiful employment for attorneys—lucrative contingency employment. But in 1987, the California Supreme Court slammed the door shut on wrongful termination suits and many states soon followed California's lead. While the beast is still alive, it's barely kicking.

How does one even think of mediating a wrongful termination situation? The employee doesn't really want to return to the job and the employer most certainly doesn't want him or her back. Perhaps there's another solution.

Presently, an employee can collect roughly six months' worth of unemployment compensation in most states before benefits run out. Those benefits are charged against the employer's reserve account, unless the employer can demonstrate that the employee quit, refused to accept suitable alternative employment with the employer, or was fired for really good cause, such as embezzlement, sexual harassment of other workers, etc.

All too often, an employee on unemployment is shortsighted. He or she goes to the unemployment office each week to pick up his or her check and submits proof of having "interviewed" at three jobs. The ex-employee really doesn't think ahead. He or she is mortified or embarrassed or angry at the former employer, the "system" and the world. The "interviews" are perfunctory, and the employee often perceives the prospective job as below his or her station. Thus the would-be employee consciously or unconsciously sabotages the interview, goes back to the unemployment office, and collects another check. While that is going on, the former employer feels like the scandalous ex-employee is stealing money from the reserve account each week.

Perhaps a change is in order.

Why not engage in a system whereby a state-hired neutral evaluator or a trained mediator hears every case of an employer-employee harassment or termination dispute as a mandatory prerequisite to the filing of an unemployment or wrongful termination claim? In such a situation, the parties can realistically focus on such issues as:

1) How long would it realistically take the employee to obtain a similar-paying job in the same or a related field (assuming such a job is available) within a reasonable geographic distance?

2) What means exist for realistic placement elsewhere within the employer's organization?

3) What means exist for cross-training the employee into another field within a reasonable period of time, with a reasonable chance that he or she will find suitable employment?

4) To what degree is the employer willing to provide financial and emotional support to the discharged employee during the time it takes to relocate the employee in a new job?

If these questions sound naïvely simplistic, consider the following:

1) Virtually no insurance company writes employer harassment or wrongful termination insurance; if they do, the premiums are astronomically high.

2) Even if the employer wins a wrongful termination suit, it will generally cost a minimum of $50,000, often several times that amount, to defend against the suit. Attorneys' fees are almost never recoverable in such an action. Plus there will be a severe disruption of work, demoralization of the work force, and permanently etched mistrust of the employer—in other words, a highly crystallized "us vs. them" mentality.

3) The employer and employee both face uncertainty. The courts have done everything possible to discourage such lawsuits, but once they get to the jury, juries have generally been very sympathetic and generous, to the poor, downtrodden worker.

This might very well be a situation where the term "millions for defense, not one dime for tribute" loses its moral—better yet, its common sense—force. Generally, a worker who truly wants to work—and most do—will find some kind of suitable employment within a year. If we assume that an average worker (dangerous word that, "average") makes $40,000 per year, then a sliding scale settlement of nine months minimum, eighteen months maximum ($30,000-$60,000) starts to look pretty reasonable from everyone's standpoint. It becomes more attractive, certainly to the employer, to treat this "outplacing period" as a time to keep the employee on the payroll, for then the money paid out, like alimony, is taxable income for the recipient, and an ordinary cost of doing business for the employer.

Does this seem more reasonable than endless litigation, the constant buildup of legal fees and the gnawing rat of uncertainty? Certainly. Is it practical? Why not? Is it better than the system we have now? Positively. Except for the only losers—the lawyers on both sides. And even they aren't losers, because the only type of lawsuit that comes close to divorce in nastiness is the harassment or wrongful termination lawsuit.

CHAPTER 12

When a Loved One Dies: Mediating Conflicts Among the Survivors

An incompetent attorney can delay a trial for months or years.
A competent attorney can delay one even longer.

– Evelle J. Younger

OFTEN A CONFLICT among wives, husbands, children, grand-children, relatives—indeed anyone who seeks to benefit financially in any way when a person is well along the road to the end we all must face, begins well before the death of the loved one.

Remember the sad tale of Mr. and Mrs. G that we discussed at the beginning of Chapter 10? While it's not common, the sad fact is that it is not **un**common, either. Brothers and sisters exhibit sibling rivalry from birth on. Sometimes it's cute, sometimes it's funny; more often it's tragic, particularly if it extends into adult-hood. There are too many "functional" dysfunctional extended families where a brother, sister, husband or wife "jockeys for posi-tion" throughout his or her whole life. Since divorce and remar-riage are common in our society, the concept of blended families has become a reality. Yet families seldom blend completely. A stepchild is never really the same as a blood child. No matter how great the love and devotion between second-time, or even third-time married mates, the old saying is true: "blood is thicker than water." Despite our best efforts to be totally equitable and fair among all our children, it's almost impossible to do so.

Usually one mate dies earlier than the other. When that happens, the natural children of the surviving mate "rally round the flagpole," often to the unconscious exclusion of the deceased mate's natural children. Although the husband and wife pledged eternal love, devotion and loyalty to each other, the children, who are often resentful that mom's or dad's place was taken by a stranger, were never part of that pledge and never wanted any part of it. Sometimes there is genuine love—or at least liking—between stepparents and stepchildren. But for the most part the children accepted the situation to keep the peace and because the new mate kept mom or dad happy. But when stepdad or stepmother is out of the picture, the rules no longer apply and it's every man or woman for himself or herself.

This occurs not only in blended families but in natural ones as well. We in the United States are, sadly, less accepting of the dignity of age than virtually any other society. If you think that's not true, think of all the senior citizens' homes that pop up in every community. Rather than have the older generation interfere with our own family lifestyles, for the most part we like them to be conveniently available, but not living with us under the same roof. For the most part, it would surprise the younger generation to find that the older folks have, if anything, even less desire to live under their children's roofs.

But a fact of life we all have to face is that unless the older generation dies at a reasonably young and vigorous age (shades of Aldous Huxley's *Brave New World*), people in their late 70s and early 80s generally start to weaken—physically and mentally. Whether it's called hardening of the arteries or Alzheimer's disease, memories fail and all too often what we euphemistically call senior citizens revert to behavior more resembling that of a petulant four-year-old child than a fully functioning adult.

The younger generation faces a Hobson's choice: Do we put the "old folks" away in a "senior citizens' community" (translation: "old age home") where they "can be professionally cared for in an atmosphere of dignity" (i.e., out of the way), or do we take the "old folks" into our homes, where we worry that they might disrupt our own lives? It's a hard choice, and you can bet that younger family members will have sharply differing opinions on the issue. Those opinions become yet more sharply divided when questions start being asked: Who is mom or dad going to live with? If mom or dad goes into a "home," who's going to pay for it if they can't afford it? The situation becomes urgent when it becomes apparent that the older folks can no longer manage in their own homes; or they can't drive a car anymore; or they can't manage a bank account or remember to pay their own bills.

Sometimes families are able to work out a livable solution between themselves. Most times, however, it involves tension. Invariably when that occurs, one or another sibling, child, mate, or whomever, believes that he or she worked harder, made greater sacrifices, and thus deserves "a little more" than the other potential beneficiaries. The jockeying for position starts subtly, almost unconsciously, and there might come a time when it is suggested that mom or dad might want to change their will, "in order to be fair." We don't want to think things like that happen, but they do.

Fortunately, most of the time, wills are not changed suddenly and on a whim. Equally fortunately, wills are seldom contested in actual practice. But when it happens, it can be as vicious and as emotionally and financially debilitating as any case I've ever seen. Family members take sides against other family members and the concept of family can be irretrievably lost.

Do lawyers make money from these types of cases? On that, I can speak from experience, for just such a case resulted in the largest jury verdict, followed by the largest settlement, and, ultimately, the largest attorney's fee I ever earned. Even though I truly believe that I earned every cent of my fee, the tragedy is that it was so unnecessary.

Here is the case. The facts are pretty much as established in front of the jury, but the names and circumstances have been changed.

Allen started a grocery business in 1939. He and his wife Arlene, who was a homemaker, had five children: Betty, Carl, Dana, Evelyn and Frank, born in that order. By 1945, Allen's business was thriving. He had added two more grocery stores, and a woman named Andrea went to work for him as a bookkeeper.

Because of her management and people skills, Allen soon pro-
moted her to manager of the largest store, while Allen assumed
the position of general manager. In 1947, Andrea suggested to
Allen that he convert his grocery stores into newfangled supermarkets. He did, and by 1949 he had a chain of five supermarkets.
Lawyer Olde suggested that he incorporate for tax and liability
purposes and Allen agreed.

In 1951, Allen's wife Arlene was diagnosed with cancer and
died. Allen and the children were devastated. By that time, the
children were at various stages. Betty had no interest whatsoever
in the business and she eventually married a stockbroker. Carl
and Dana, natural entrepreneurs, accepted their father's invitation
to work for him. While he was a hard taskmaster, the two boys
took to the supermarket business like ducks to water. Evelyn went
through a particularly hard teenage period. She was wild, the
"black sheep" of the family, and she really didn't give a damn
what the rest thought. As for Frank, he was ten years old and a
bundle of fun and energy.

Four years later, Allen announced that he had been alone long
enough, and that he and Andrea had decided to "tie the knot."
The children were not happy, feeling that a stranger was crawling
into their mother's bed, but they bore up stoically. They never
called her "mom" or even "stepmom." She remained "Andrea."

The business continued to grow. By 1960, Allen had fifteen
supermarkets and more money than anyone could ever hope to
spend. He felt his sons Carl and Dana had worked hard, and due
to their efforts, they should have "a little extra." He "sold" each of
them 4 percent of the stock in his company, Allen's Supermarkets,
Inc., for $1.00 each. Remember this, as it will become important.
His plan was that as the other children got older, he'd work them
into the business as well, and one day they'd all be more or less
equal. The marriage to Andrea was very successful. She and Allen
continued to work side by side and their relationship was vibrant
and endlessly romantic.

By 1972, lawyer Olde was slowing down. Allen felt it was time
for him and Andrea to take some time off. Betty and her husband
were independently wealthy, Evelyn had still not "gotten her act

together," and Allen thought he'd give young Frank a chance at managing one of the smaller markets to see how he did at handling the responsibility. Carl and Dana became general managers of the entire chain. Under their management, business continued to boom. They convinced dad that the old company accountant, Bob Crotchett, now 78 years old, was a fossil. They had met Herb Hotshot, a brash, young accountant, at the weekly Jaycee meeting, and he was "with it"—translation, Herb thought as they did and was amenable to "bending the rules a bit" to help the family avoid taxes as much as possible.

Before long, Crotchett was put out to pasture and Herb was a fixture at the Allen's Supermarket headquarters. Herb, Carl and Dana became ever closer friends. They took trips to Europe together, went to Superbowl games, even became partners in a time-share at Cabo San Lucas in Baja California. Best of all, since the Allen's Supermarket Corporation had meetings and research inspections of facilities in other countries, the travel expenses could be written off on taxes.

Meanwhile, Allen was enjoying his golden years, now that "the boys" were taking care of business. They'd added two more stores to the chain and things continued to get bigger and better. His old friend, attorney Olde, now in the fullness of his years, was about to retire from the practice. As a last gift to Allen, he wanted to make sure his legal house was in order. Allen had always talked about wanting to provide for Andrea, to make certain that during her lifetime she had everything she wanted and more. And when she passed away, he wanted to make sure that his bounty passed equally to all five of his children.

Olde was a general practitioner, but he had access to some fill-in-the-blank trust forms from the 1950s. In order to save on death taxes and probate, he told Allen, a trust was essential. And the will that accompanied the trust would simply "pour over" anything outside the trust into the trust.

"Whatever you say, Olde," Allen remarked. "You're the lawyer. I assume you know your business and wouldn't steer me wrong." So Allen and Andrea executed a trust. Neither of them knew much about the law and they hardly glanced at the 79-page document before signing it. They were on their way to Hawaii the next day and couldn't be bothered.

A year later, Olde passed on. Since Allen's Supermarket Corporation was a large business, it was inconceivable that it could function without a lawyer—a general counsel. But since Allen had already turned most of the day-to-day operation over to Carl and Dana, he turned the selection of a new lawyer over to them, too. "Herb," they said, with a smile and a wink, "you know how we think. Can you find us a lawyer?"

"Of course," said Herb. He immediately located Youngblood, an eager, very compliant lawyer who had just become an associate in a middle-sized firm and was overwhelmed that he would even be considered as general counsel to the wealthy, famous Allen's Supermarket chain. "Just so long as you know who's **really** in control of Allen's," Herb told him, "you'll do just fine."

As time went on, the aged Allen became ill with cancer. His mind started to wander and he found it difficult to concentrate on business. Herb and Youngblood approached Allen one day and told him, "We're certain that Olde meant nothing but the best for you, but that was many years ago. Tax laws have changed and the value of your Allen's Supermarket stock has gone up so high that unless you find a way to cap its value, the taxes on your estate will be so much that no one but the government will end up getting anything."

Obviously, that had the desired effect on Allen, who, though sick, did not want his wife and children to go without. "What must I do?" he asked his trusted advisers.

"You must recapitalize the corporation," they said. "You now own 92 percent of Allen's Supermarket—92 shares of common stock in the company. You should trade in your ninety-two shares of common stock for ninety-two *hundred* shares of **preferred** stock in the company, We'll fix the value of that stock at $2 million. That way, the value of the preferred stock will always be $2 million, no matter what happens to the company, and that will be the value of your estate, period."

"Isn't that illegal?" Allen asked. "Can you really do that?"

"It's perfectly legal," Youngblood replied. "It's done all the time. Even better, we'll strengthen your position in the company by making it **voting** preferred stock for as long as you live."

"That sounds kind of silly," Allen said. "I already own 92 percent of the company. Carl and Dana know what I want and I've always been able to run the company exactly the way I want. Why is it necessary to give me even more voting power?"

"Let's just say everyone realizes who you are and what you've accomplished. And everyone wants you to be not only the president, but the chairman emeritus of the board as well."

"OK, you guys know what you're doing. Just bring me the papers to sign when you're ready." And Allen drifted off to sleep.

A week later, Herb and Youngblood brought a slew of paperwork to Allen and Andrea to sign. Under the contract, Allen traded in his 92 shares of common stock for 9,200 shares of preferred stock with voting rights "as long as Allen is alive, with a fixed value of $2 million." Andrea was a little suspicious because the right to vote the stock ended with Allen's death, but Allen, who was too exhausted to read and understand what was written, said, "Just sign it." Besides, she trusted that the family would stay together and work together, so she signed the papers. Next, there was an amendment to the family trust. Instead of holding 92 shares of common stock, the trust now held 9,200 shares of preferred stock. The only part of the trust that Allen and Andrea carefully re-read was the part that said that on Allen's death Andrea would be taken care of from the property in the trust and that on Andrea's demise the trust would be equally divided among Allen's five children. Everything seemed to be in perfect order. When Herb and Youngblood saw Carl and Dana in the hall, they smiled broadly and remarked, "OK, guys, now you own the company."

Allen's condition worsened. In October of that year he died. Although Allen's Supermarket Corporation was worth $20 million, Andrea was assured she need not worry, since Allen's taxable estate, tied to the value of the preferred stock, was only worth $2 million.

"So you mean we get 92 percent of the other $18,000,000 tax-free?" Andrea asked Youngblood. "How is that possible?"

"Well, um, no…it's not exactly that way," Youngblood stammered.

Slowly the horror of what had happened came out.

Corporations generally issue two kinds of stock: common stock and preferred stock. Which do you think is more valuable? Which would you rather have? If preferred stock is truly "preferred," it must be much better and more valuable that mere "common" stock, right? To use Youngblood's words, "Well, um, no. It's not exactly that way."

Preferred stock is more like a debt instrument than a true share in the company. It is set at a certain value and generally pays fixed dividends. But the basic value of that stock will never go up (unless it's traded on the open market). Thus, Allen's "preferred" stock was worth $2 million *and not one cent more,* regardless of the value of the corporation. Preferred stock is "preferred" only in the sense that the owners of the preferred stock will get paid before the owners of common stock if the company is in shaky financial shape.

Once the preferred stock is taken care of, the rest of the equity in the company is divided among the holders of common stock. In Allen's case, his preferred stock had the absolute right to preference on the first $2 million of the value of the corporation. That left $18 million worth of value in the company which, of course, would be equally divided among Allen's children, right? Wrong. The **$2 million** would be equally divided—$400,000 each. And the $18 million?

Remember back in 1960, when Allen "sold" 4 percent of his common stock to Carl and 4 percent to Dana for $1.00 each? Carl and Dana never converted **their** common stock to preferred stock. So now, instead of owning 8 percent of the common stock in Allen's Supermarket Corporation, they each owned 50 percent of the common stock in the company. And since Allen's right to vote his stock terminated on his death, they now exercised *100 percent of the voting control of the company.*

Since Allen's Supermarket represented virtually all of the value of Allen's estate, his wishes for equal distribution to all five of his children after Andrea died looked like this:

Betty	=	$ 400,000	(2 percent of the estate)
Carl	=	$ 9,400,000	(47 percent of the estate)
Dana	=	$ 9,400,000	(47 percent of the estate)
Evelyn	=	$ 400,000	(2 percent of the estate)
Frank	=	$ 400,000	(2 percent of the estate)

Even worse, Andrea had a "pot" of $2 million to sustain her for the rest of her life, and once that was gone, it was just too bad. If she used up any or all of that money, the percentage that Carl and Dana would ultimately receive would be even larger than their combined 94 percent of Allen's estate.

Carl and Dana immediately took the position: "That's what Dad wanted, or he wouldn't have signed the papers. We're sorry that the rest of you are not getting what we got, but you have to realize that we worked in the business every day for many years." Accountant Herb and lawyer Youngblood backed up Carl's and Dana's side of the story, which was not unexpected, since they were still on the staff of Allen's Supermarket Corporation and were being paid *very* well.

Betty, the oldest child and always the peacemaker of the family, tried to suggest a series of compromises, but Carl and Dana would hear none of it. Evelyn figured life was tough anyway, and what had happened could not be rectified. Andrea fumed, had a heart attack, and was hospitalized within six months after Allen's death. And young Frank? He retained me on a contingency basis. Carl and Dana, irritated that Frank would dare challenge his father's "carefully executed" estate plan, immediately fired Frank from his job as manager of two of the market's better stores. All attempts at mediation broke down.

I won't make the horror story more horrible than it needs to be, and I won't divulge the result of the jury trial, which consumed six weeks from start to finish after six years of legal wrangling among four different "sides" and an army of lawyers, or the secondary litigation against Herb, Youngblood and others, which finally ended up nine years after Allen's death. I will only say that the lawsuits ended up costing the parties a combined total of more than $5 million, not counting the recovery, all of which came out of Allen's estate. They also left a law firm in bankruptcy, and permanently shattered family relations for perhaps generations to come.

Although I do not suggest that this ugly scenario makes for a "fun" parlor game, might I suggest that you and a series of friends, associates, or even lawyers get together to try to formulate a practical solution to the Allen problem? In order to make it realistic, we'll need the following "players."

1. Carl and Dana
2. Andrea
3. Betty
4. Evelyn
5. Frank
6. Herb and Youngblood
7. A mediator.

The basic facts are as they appear above. You can always add little touches to the characters to give them depth. For example, assume Evelyn is living in a $500 per month apartment, her husband has abandoned her and she has two children; she got into drugs and is now on rehabilitation and welfare. Carl is going through a vicious divorce in which his wife's attorney sees his part of Allen's bounty as community property and feels that Carl's soon-to-be-ex-wife is entitled to 50 percent of anything Carl gets. Betty is worth $10 million in her own right. Andrea is put on life support at a cost of $10,000 a day. The possibilities are limited only by your own creativity.

The purpose of this exercise is to demonstrate that people must be willing to be flexible, to talk, and to consider the legal and emotional costs that are certain to occur if they *don't* talk and make allowances for mistakes. And perhaps to remember that family is the closest unit most of us have in the world. Finally, to know that one way or the other, no matter how much money or property is involved, we can't take it with us when we go.

CHAPTER 13

Expanding Conflict Management Techniques to Every Field of Human Conflict

A law firm is more successful when it has
more clients than partners.

– Henny Youngman

A lawyer is a man who induces two other men to strip for a fight
and then runs off with their clothes.

– Anonymous

N OUR PRESENT SYSTEM, disputes are resolved "on the court-house steps" by a forced compromise—a resolution that is called a "good settlement" if both sides are equally unhappy. It doesn't have to be that way. In a mediated situation, where both sides constructively work out their differences, negotiations can lead to win-win situations in every sphere of human conflict.

Thus far, we have dealt with mediation and conflict resolution in divorces and contracts, two of the most bitter and sensitive types of conflict.

Numerically, the greatest number of cases filed in the courts today are personal injury cases—primarily automobile accidents, followed by professional malpractice cases and debt collection cases. All too often they result in bankruptcy with the creditor getting virtually nothing after spending substantial sums on litigation.

For years, personal injury has been the great lottery in our society. Satirized in Billy Wilder's motion picture, *The Fortune Cookie* several years ago, the practice, if anything, has gotten worse.

In the 1960s a lawyer's rule of thumb was that you settled a case for "three to five times medical specials."

The client was rear-ended and suffered a whiplash injury—medically called a cervical sprain or strain. He or she went through neck pain and stiffness, saw an orthopedist, walked around in a neck brace for some time, and underwent physical therapy—usually tugs, pulleys and weights—for about three months. The bill usually came to somewhere between $1,000 and $1,500 and the case would usually settle for three to five times that amount. The lawyer got one-third of the recovery, the health-care providers were paid, and the remainder, usually about one-third of the total, went to the client—tax free, since it was compensation for personal injury.

It was relatively easy. Lawyers looked at it as the "fat" of the practice. Tempers rarely frayed. If you couldn't settle a case, you tried it fairly quickly.

Some accident victims were horribly injured from major incidents. Those cases occasionally resulted in million-dollar verdicts. For the most part, though, it was "three to five times specials" for soft tissue injuries and "five to seven times specials" for "objective" injuries such as broken bones.

Let's not kid ourselves. Despite the jokes about whiplash injuries, they are very real and can be very painful. The mechanics of the body may explain why. Ask anyone how much they think the human head weighs. They'll probably give answers ranging from five to ten pounds. The answer is that the human head weighs closer to twenty pounds—about as much as a bowling ball. It doesn't feel heavy because it's supported by large muscles.

Ask that same person how large the spine is. Most people, believing that the spinal cord includes the vertebrae that support it, will estimate it has a diameter of two inches or so. In fact, the spinal cord itself has the diameter of a pencil.

Thus we have a bowling ball sitting atop a pencil—well protected by a series of interlocking muscles and vertebrae—but nevertheless not a very secure platform. Most orthopedic surgeons agree that man was not naturally constructed to walk upright on two legs and because we walk in a way we weren't designed to, we subject our bodies every day of our lives to severe pressures that result in degenerative disc disease.

When we are involved in an automobile accident—particularly one in which we are struck from the rear—the "bowling ball" of our head is dislodged for a split second from the "pencil" of our spine. Instinct tells the body that one is not going to survive very long without the other. The head and spinal cord seek to return to position as quickly as possible. The counterforce causes the head and spine to "whip" through a lot of soft tissue—fatty tissue, unused muscles, blood vessels, and, most important, nerves.

Nerve cells transmit message signals throughout the body. Without them, you'd never feel pain if you cut yourself. You could lose a leg and never know it. A child first learns that fire is dangerous when he touches a hot stove. He wouldn't acquire that knowledge without nerve cells. In order to transmit signals, nerve cells use electrical impulses. Each one **almost** touches the next. There's a space between them—the synaptic gap—so small it can't be seen by the most powerful microscope. Not every signal successfully crosses the tiny gap. Those that do race on to the next nerve cell. The journey continues more than a million times until the signal reaches the brain. The entire series of transmissions takes less than a thousandth of a second.

When the head and spine race back toward one another, they irritate soft tissue and nerves. The soft tissue swells, pushing against the nerves. The nerves react by having a spasm. The result is pain and stiffness. Unlike a wound on the surface of the skin, the area inside the base of the neck is constricted. A cut finger may take a week to heal. In the confining atmosphere of the neck and back, healing is a much slower process.

Depending on the severity of the injury, most whiplash injuries take two to three months to heal. Some heal quicker, while other victims may suffer legitimate pain for as long as two years. Because of arthritic changes—degenerative disc disease—the injured neck or back will probably never be what it was before the accident.

Nevertheless, once the public learned about the "three to five times special damages" formula, it didn't take long for them to figure out that if you could get $3,000 for $1,000 worth of treatment, you could get $6,000 to $10,000 if you received $2,000 worth of treatment. That realization, coupled with the fact that many orthopedic surgeons were too busy to spend time on what they considered a relatively minor injury or simply stopped working on backs and necks because of the increased risk of medical malpractice claims, led to a proliferation of chiropractors, acupuncturists, osteopaths, holistic healers, and a wide range of physical therapists coming to specialize in soft tissue injury.

I do not harbor ill will against the chiropractic fraternity. On the contrary, I have experienced severe back pain myself, and I believe the relief obtained from chiropractors is heaven-sent. But all too frequently, chiropractors have been willing to treat soft-tissue injuries on a daily or even twice-daily basis, "manipulating the spine" to relieve tension and compression pain. Bills mount up rapidly. Before you know it, there can be more than $3,000 worth of chiropractic bills.

Insurance companies prey on the general public's belief that a medical doctor is a "real" doctor and a chiropractor is a glorified witch doctor. The insurance companies, which defend the allegedly guilty party in automobile accident cases, hardly ever use the services of a chiropractor. Rather, their so-called "independent" expert is likely to be an orthopedic surgeon or a neurosurgeon with a pedigree longer than that of an AKC purebred champion wolfhound. You may rest assured that the expert will downgrade the role of the chiropractor. In thirty-three years of practice, I have yet to hear a doctor testifying for the defense refer to a chiropractor as "Doctor Smith." It is invariably, "Chiropractor Smith" or "Osteopath Smith," who, "by his manipulation actually exacerbated an injury that should have cured itself in six weeks."

The games played on both sides of the personal injury lawsuit are costly and unnecessary.

There are several ways to cure the problem.

1) Limit the plaintiff's lawyer's fees to 25 percent of the net recovery.

California recently proposed an "anti-lawyer" initiative that would have slashed contingent fees to 25 percent of the first $100,000 recovered, 15 percent of the next $100,000 recovered, and 10 percent of everything over $200,000. When the trial lawyers threatened to expose how the major insurance companies, proponents of the initiative, had been sued and found guilty of bad faith on several occasions, there was a cry of outrage from the insurance interests about how the trial lawyers had "screwed the public again." Yet, thereafter the insurance companies somehow lost interest in putting big money behind the initiative and it ultimately did not pass.

I believe such a cut is too drastic, for it would drive the "heavy hitters" as well as the "mills" out of business, and the little man would be left without protection in a situation where he suffered legitimate, serious injuries through another person's fault. But I also believe that the lawyer who takes 45 percent of the gross recovery is stealing from the client and from the public. Given the relatively simple mechanical procedures involved in personal injury law, I feel that a straight 25 percent of the net recovery, after payment of the doctor's bills, is appropriate and fair.

2) Pop the balloon of false expectations.

We must rid ourselves of the "lottery mentality" that pushes every injured person into the arms of the nearest personal injury lawyer. The outmoded "three to five times specials" formula must be dropped in favor of a more case-specific recovery.

We might consider a recovery that is related to (but not invariably based on) the percentage of permanent disability. For example, the loss of an arm would be equivalent to x percent of permanent disability, which would equal x amount of money, and the loss of a finger would be equivalent to y percent of permanent disability, amounting to y dollars, regardless of the amount spent for medical care.

That might be a starting point toward giving an injured person and the insurance carrier a reasonable expectation of what the ultimate recovery would be.

3) Take personal injury cases out of the hands of juries.
That is probably the most controversial proposal I make in this entire book, and one which will earn me the disdain of colleagues on both sides of personal injury cases. How dare I deny litigants their constitutional right to trial by jury?

It is historically self-evident that juries made up of lay people can be swayed by artful rhetoric far more easily than can a judge. A combination of the percentage of permanent disability with reasonable consideration for pain and suffering, coupled with a judge administering personal injury cases would result, at least theoretically, in far greater predictability than we now face.

4) Use a completely independent, state-paid group of physicians to treat and evaluate the injuries.
Virtually all managed health-care systems use "gatekeepers"—primary care practitioners who determine whether or not a patient needs more specialized care than the gatekeeper can provide—because of the necessity to ration health care. By extending the idea to accident-related personal injuries, we would be taking the first step in assuring there would be a truly independent group of health-care providers who were neither paid by the insurance carriers nor by plaintiff's legal counsel.

That would go a long way toward giving the injured person a realistic appraisal of his or her care, treatment, and recovery (both physically and monetarily) and would change the lottery concept with which too many lawyers and their clients approach accident-related personal injuries today.

5) Institute a *fair* "no fault" program.
When insurance companies gave up the ghost on their proposed no fault political bills, they swung the pendulum all the way to the other side: if it was a trial the plaintiffs' attorneys wanted, a trial they would get—in virtually every case where the

injured party refused to accept the insurance company's often unreasonably low offer.

That brought the injured plaintiff who could not afford substantial lawyer's fees right back to where he or she was in the 1950s. Plaintiffs' personal injury lawyers loved personal injury practice when it was "shaking the tree and picking the plums up off the ground."

Now, however, a new menace faces plaintiffs' lawyers and their hapless clients: generally speaking, where liability is clear, a soft-tissue case (one where there are no broken bones) is worth somewhere between $3,500 and $15,000 (the broadest possible average taken from national "Jury Verdicts Weekly" sheets and from discussions among hundreds of lawyers who represent both plaintiffs bar and defendants). The median settlement figure is between $5,000 and $7,500. That means, if the lawyer gets a third of the gross recovery, he or she would get between $1,667 and $2,500, which is fine so long as the lawyer's actual work time on the case does not exceed seven to ten hours.

The insurance companies, whose lawyers are paid indirectly by every policyholder who buys insurance from that particular company, and which have virtually unlimited funds (do you ever wonder who builds most of the largest buildings in any city?), have made it known that they will "go the distance." It is a rule of thumb that it will take a lawyer a **minimum** of 50 hours to get to and through a short (one-to-two-day) trial, perhaps two or three times that in a case where liability is hotly contested.

To further compound the difficulties of the situation, juries today are invariably instructed on comparative negligence, which means that if the plaintiff (the injured party) is 10 percent at fault, his recovery from a jury is to be reduced by 10 percent. A $15,000 verdict where a claimant is held to be one-third at fault quickly dissolves into a $10,000 verdict.

The average lawyer believes that he or she is worth $200 to $250 per hour—some much more, some a little less. That's pretty much the going rate for a non-contingency business lawyer. If a lawyer is at the low end of the scale, at $200 per hour, and has to work 50 hours to get a personal injury contingency case through trial, no matter how slight the injury, he or she must make $10,000 in fees or risk losing that amount on non-contingency billings. And unlike hourly billings, contingency cases are never a sure thing, so the contingency fee lawyer has a certain risk factor involved.

In order to make a $10,000 fee, the lawyer must get a $30,000 settlement. But he or she is faced with the greatest likelihood that a jury verdict will be between $5,000 and $7,500. Using the $7,500 figure, the lawyer would get $2,500, or $50 per hour—one fourth of what he or she would charge an hourly client.

No matter what, attorneys have fixed office expenses, and if they aren't met, the lawyer must close his or her doors and go flip burgers at the local McDonald's. That's not a particularly attractive alternative.

What happens? The number of lawyers willing to take a plaintiff's case on a contingency basis dries up pretty rapidly. The superior economic muscle of the insurance companies deprives claimants of a fair opportunity to be heard and to recover a just and fair damage award—actually, if not strictly legally speaking.

Most advertising (paid for by insurance carriers and those who work for their interests) are quick to blame "the powerful trial lawyers' lobby" for sabotaging the "no fault" system—a system where a person injured in an accident obtains financial payment without the concept of "fault." On its face, it sounds like a fair and equitable system. It would eliminate the courtroom aspects that make personal injury law so expensive today. The insurance companies tell us it would cut premiums and result in faster delivery and better services for everyone in the country.

So why hasn't the "no fault" system been passed by every state legislature? And why have the trial lawyers fought against it so vigorously? Primarily because the public has realized that, as proposed by the insurance companies, "no fault" is **no fair**. An injured person would promptly receive reimbursement for his or her **medical** expenses, but there would be severe limits on recovery for pain and suffering, loss of income, decreased earning capacity, or any other intangibles that interrupt one's life when one is seriously injured.

The way to cure the turmoil over "no fault" would be to make it truly no fault and truly fair for everyone concerned.

Representatives of the insurance industry and representatives of the trial lawyers' associations could meet with a qualified mediator and arrive at a resolution that would be in everyone's reasonable best interests. The only thing on which we can all agree at this point is that the present system doesn't work, it's costly and ineffective, and it spreads seeds of discontent that create a "get it while you can" atmosphere.

Having suggested these framework ideas for revolutionizing the system, we should move to the next step: mediation in the event that a personal injury plaintiff's attorney and the insurance carrier cannot come to agreement.

The idea of competing health-care experts is a waste of everyone's time. A mediator might suggest, for example, that the injured person be examined (the cost of which would be paid for equally by both sides) by the **mediator's** expert. That expert would report back to the parties and the mediator, and the process would then move on to its next logical step.

Under our present system, once a case is settled, it is settled for good and for ever. If the injured party needs future medical care, he or she must pay for it out of his or her own pocket (or by way of his or her own health insurance). While that represents "closure" for the insurance carrier settling the case, the plaintiff's lawyer invariably builds an extra amount into the settlement for unanticipated future medical expenses, whether or not they ever eventuate.

That philosophy is unhealthy: it promotes distrust between the injured party and the other party's insurance carrier, because the plaintiff feels (justifiably) that the defendant's insurance company looks upon him or her as just another number—and a greedy one at that—seeking to soak the company for whatever her or she can get while the getting is good.

It would be healthier if the mediator convinced the parties that the defendant's insurance carrier could pay less now, but extend medical coverage benefits for an indefinite period of time, provided the injured party used agreed-upon doctors. That would mean a cost saving for everyone and would help the injured party feel that he or she is not just being "dumped" at the earliest moment.

The mediator might suggest other alternatives to assist both parties, such as vocational rehabilitation, paid for by the insurance carrier, or supplemental income for a time to compensate the injured party for lost income.

As in all other fields, personal injury law creates opportunities for constructive problem resolution. When the problems resolve themselves, lawyers' fees on both sides are saved and we move into a more cooperative realm of managing conflict in our society.

Another field in which litigation has run rampant is debt collection.

A generation ago, it was not the serious problem it is today. Bankruptcy was marginally more popular than suicide. During the Great Depression years, many folks attempted suicide rather than face the shame of "going bankrupt."

Not today.

Nowadays, companies from Texaco Oil to Continental Airlines, Greyhound Bus Lines to Johns-Manville and Dow Corning have filed for bankruptcy protection (note how we've subtly changed the use of the words) and, without seriously besmirching their reputations, emerged more financially powerful than ever. Continental got rid of its unions; Texaco got rid of a major judgment; Greyhound discharged thousands of extraneous employees and millions of dollars worth of debt; Johns-Manville got rid of thousands of asbestosis lawsuits before they ever came to trial; and myriad breast implant cases were suddenly—forcibly—resolved by the setting up of a single, omnibus settlement fund.

It has been estimated that in any given year since 1980, America has discharged 5 percent of its obligations through bankruptcy proceedings. Doesn't sound like much, does it? In 1990, that amounted to $270 billion or about $1,250 for every man, woman and child in the United States.

Someone has to take the "hit" for that. Usually, it's all of us in the guise of increased consumer prices, more difficulty in borrowing money, and higher interest rates.

With the advent of the credit card, Americans have learned to live on credit in a big way. Even national politicians have told us that we've mortgaged our children's future through our intemperate spending and borrowing. We want the better life and we want it **now.** If a 36-inch TV screen sits in the neighbor's home, we want a 42-inch screen in ours and we want it **today.** If we can't afford it, God created VISA and MasterCard. The Chevrolet that used to cost $2,500 now costs $20,000, and we usually don't have that kind of cash on hand, because we've forgotten how to save money for something we want. Even supermarkets are now taking credit cards.

The problem is that after a while we've spent not only beyond our means, but beyond our reasonable ability to repay the loans. Credit card companies, department stores and oil companies love it when we make minimum payments, because they are charging anywhere from 18 to 24 percent per annum interest on the money we owe them. It's not unusual for the car we've bought or leased on time to cost two or three times what it would have cost had we paid cash. Although every state has laws against usury, they do not apply to the purchase of goods on time or to credit card companies.

One day we find that we are unable to make the minimum payment. The friendly credit card company turns decidedly hostile and threatens to report us to the credit reporting agencies. They warn us that once we have bad credit, we will not be able to borrow from anyone. Suddenly the door to the toy store is closed. What's more, the proprietor of that store—the credit card company—has locked the door. Too late we learn there's a price for all the toys we've bought, which are now beyond the warranty period, are in need of repairs, and are no longer "state of the art."

Debt collection practice is a most horrid experience for the debtor. Although they don't have debtor's prisons anymore, the humiliation is almost as bad. After the lawyer for the collection agency sends you two or three "You'd better pay or else!" form letters, you find yourself being sued. It is almost impossible to avoid judgment in such a case, because you did sign a contract, you got the goods, and you owe the money.

Once there is a judgment against you, the indignities mount. The creditor files an abstract of judgment, attaching to any real property you own, including your house. The creditor's lawyer hauls you in for a judgment debtor's examination. You are taken into a small room where, under oath, you must disclose every asset and liability you have. I have seen cases where a lawyer has asked a hapless judgment debtor to empty out his wallet and take off his watch, right then and there—and the lawyer legally seized the items.

While there are protections against harassment, and while not everything you own can be taken away from you, going through post-judgment procedures are among life's most humiliating and debilitating experiences. The crisis comes on the day you write a check on your bank account and it bounces because the judgment creditor has attached (grabbed) all the money in the account, without even letting you know. Or on the day when you expect your paycheck and find that the judgment creditor has garnished (grabbed) it from your employer before reached you.

Ultimately, you veer closer and closer to bankruptcy. If you are like most people—and unlike Continental Airlines, etc.—it is something you dread more than anything, except for death, divorce, or serious illness.

Is there a reasonable solution? I believe there is.

Even in this distressing situation, mediation can be helpful for both the creditor and the distraught debtor. The last thing the creditors really want is for the debtor to file bankruptcy, because then they will either get nothing or get a very small percentage of what is owed. The remainder of the debt is discharged. The creditor loses any bargaining power he might have had, because once a bankruptcy appears on the debtor's credit record, it can't get any worse.

Let's assume that instead of going to the courts and the credit reporting agencies, the creditor suggests mediation under the auspices of an experienced credit counselor.

The debtor reveals all of his other mounting debts. The mediator invites all the creditors to participate in the mediation. Constructive resolution is bound to occur.

For example, all parties might agree that for a period of six months, a year, or even longer, the debtor would not make any new purchases or borrow any funds without an agreement between himself and his creditors, after discussion with the mediator. During the first six months, payments on the existing debts, except for necessities such as rent or house payments, utility bills, and food, would be suspended and all or a substantial part of the interest would stop accruing, while the debtor builds up a savings account, held in trust by a trustee. That account would be used to pay for reasonable costs of living in accordance with a budget agreed to by the debtor and his creditors. That budget need not be Draconian. It may include reasonable allowances for very minor luxuries. But it would force the debtor to stop profligate spending and put a certain amount each month into the trust savings account.

At the end of a predetermined period, the trustee would issue pro-rata payments to the creditors. Thereafter, the debtor and the trustee would calculate a reasonable distribution to be made each month to the creditors. At the end of each month, the trustee would make those payments. Whether the debts would then draw full interest, no interest, or partial interest would be determined by the debtor, the creditors, and the mediator. The creditors would agree that so long as the debtor was making the agreed payments, there would be no adverse credit reports, and if the debtor made all payments on the program, they would give him a favorable credit report.

This method would create a "win" for everyone concerned. The debtor would avoid lawsuits, the creditor would get paid, and the debtor ultimately would learn fiscal responsibility from the sad adventure.

Several suitable alternatives may be available. That would be a matter for the creditors, the debtor, and the mediator. But as long as the parties agreed to act in their own best interests, and so long as those interests ultimately joined, there would be nothing that couldn't be done.

Let's extend mediation to the next angriest litigation after divorce: professional malpractice.

The relationship between a professional and his or her client or patient is fiduciary in nature. That means the professional owes his or her client or patient the highest duty of good faith, fair dealing, open communication, and professionalism. When such a relationship sours, the client or patient has blood in his eye and murder in his heart. More than in any other relationship except marriage—which is also characterized as fiduciary—the subordinate party, the client or patient, has put trust and confidence in the professional. There is hell to pay when the client perceives that that trust has been betrayed.

Yet doctors and lawyers suffer from the same disease as the rest of us: they are human and they make mistakes.

While there is the occasional, very rare individual who knows he or she is betraying a patient's or client's interests, most professionals really do try their hardest to justify the trust of their patients or clients and to do the job they believe must be done.

A doctor may amputate the wrong limb. A lawyer may let the statute of limitations lapse, thereby barring a client's recovery, before he or she remembers to file the lawsuit. These are clear instances of an error or omission (the common word is malpractice).

But there are many more cases where, despite the professional's best efforts, patients die on the operating table, there are complications, or a cancer is not diagnosed in time. An expert witness may not testify the way the lawyer expected. The judge or jury may rule against the client.

Do these things mean there has been malpractice? Generally not. But they become malpractice cases when the doctor, lawyer, or other professional, usually out of fear or misplaced guilt, neglects to confront the situation directly and explain to the client or patient exactly what happened and why. If there **cannot** be an explanation, the professional can sympathetically and understandingly address that problem with the patient or client and hopefully resolve—at least in the client's or patient's mind—what the professional thinks **might** have happened to cause the unfavorable result.

In all my years of practice, I have found that perhaps 10 percent of clients who have approached me to take on a malpractice case really do have a legitimate claim against their professional practitioner. I have spoken with numerous defense attorneys—lawyers representing professionals who have been sued—and they strongly concur with my opinion that more than 90 percent of the so-called malpractice cases do not involve an actual situation where the professional fell below the accepted standard of care.

The vast majority of malpractice cases involve failure to communicate—outlining the risks **before** the professional takes on the case or the surgery—and making certain that the communication lines are open before, during, and after the event for which the professional is retained.

There is a reverse side to this picture. In law, for example, the client hires a lawyer to win the case, and the client sees the facts so clearly delineated that he or she feels the case is an absolute winner. If the client does not get what, in his or her mind is a clear-cut "win," the client believes that the **lawyer** lost the case. How could the lawyer **not** have won the case, when the facts were so clear? Thus, it **must** have been the **lawyer** who screwed up the case. That's the only way the debacle could have happened. Accordingly, the client believes, the lawyer should not be paid.

Even in a situation where the lawyer "wins" the case, if there's a bill outstanding when the case is over and there is not going to be a continuing attorney-client relationship, woe be to the lawyer. The curve of appreciation for the professional's efforts diminishes in direct correlation to the amount of time that passes with the bill still outstanding.

On the first day after the case is over, the client crows about how the attorney is the best in the world and what a brilliant victory the lawyer scored. After a month, the lawyer has become "pretty good, but I still owe him a little too much money." Another month goes by. "Well, the lawyer might have won the case, but it was pretty easy. After all, the facts were right there, and **any** lawyer—even one that was much more reasonable (interesting word, that)—would have won the case." After yet another month: "You know, that sonofagun is still trying to collect money from me after **I** had to try most of the case **myself!**"

The moment the lawyer tries to enforce his or her fee agreement, the client immediately threatens to bring a malpractice action or go to the State Bar, threats that are very real and frightening to the average practitioner.

It is not so great a problem in the medical profession, since doctors usually make certain medical insurance is available before they even take on a patient. Still, a complaint to a state agency governing professional practice is not pleasant, and a malpractice suit, even if totally unjustified, must be reported to the state's licensing agency.

Mediation as a means of opening lines of communication between professional and client or patient is a worthwhile tool. If 90 percent of malpractice cases don't involve malpractice, but rather a lack of communication, mediation would theoretically eliminate 90 percent of such lawsuits before they were ever filed.

I suggest that before being allowed to file an action for malpractice—or, in the case of a professional, prior to a professional being allowed to file a lawsuit to enforce a claim for fees—the client or patient and the professional involved first be required to go to a mediation clinic operated by the state or county. In order to disabuse the nonprofessional that he is walking into a "set up," none of the mediators involved should be members of the profession in the controversy. But the mediator must have immediate and continuing access to professionals in the field whose credentials—particularly with reference to patient or client relations— are impeccable: a retired judge, a member of the governing board of accountancy, etc.

The purpose of the mediation, as in every other field of endeavor, is to get people talking: to have each side vent their fears and frustrations, their expectations and their disappointments. Once the anger and fear have abated, once the client or patient realizes that the professional is only a human being with a title, and once the professional recognizes that perhaps he or she could have done a better job of communicating, the opposing sides can start to come together constructively, each to achieve his or her own best interests.

That may not always be as easy as it sounds. A manufacturer or a retailer sells a product that can usually be replaced. A restaurateur can make up for a poor meal with a free meal later to an offended customer.

A professional, on the other hand, has nothing to sell but his time and talent. Time spent by the professional, particularly one engaged in a small legal or accounting firm, cannot be recaptured, nor billed to others, and the professional relies on a steady income stream to enable him or her to live. Giving up a substantial fee may truly mean the difference between a reasonable paycheck and going without pay for a month.

However, a professional is the first to realize that spending time defending a malpractice lawsuit, whether or not it is well-founded, will consume even more billable time and more emotional expense that cannot be retrieved. Thus it becomes incumbent upon the professional to approach mediation with a good-faith attitude of doing what is in his or her best interests.

What about the malpractice action that really **is** malpractice, which has resulted in substantial damages to the client?

Those, too, are amenable to resolution through conflict management and mediation. In the event of medical malpractice, which usually has severe and life-affecting results, the federal, state, or local government should provide lifetime care for the injured person, paid for out of a mandatory pool funded by professionals themselves. In the case of legal, accounting, or other professional malpractice, the profession involved might likewise have a monetary pool funded through the State Bar, Board of Accountancy, etc. That might even be extended by way of a public surtax or assessment to insure coverage for all professional calamities.

The spreading of risk to the greatest possible number of people would result in an actual cost of fewer dollars per person than we are now paying to achieve much less in the way of justice.

And when we spent dollars to cure our legal addiction rather than increase it, we are making a move in the right direction.

And While We're Waiting for the System to Change: Fifteen Practical Ways You Can Cut Your Lawyers' Fees In Half— Or More

"The laws I love. The lawyers I suspect."

– Charles Churchill

S THE SYSTEM going to change immediately? Not as long as it is entrenched and the lawyers are the only ones licensed to practice law. (And legislators, who are mostly lawyers, have made certain that there are criminal penalties for those who try to represent others without such a license).

But there's no law against representing yourself, and I can tell you from bitter experience that the toughest cases I've ever tried have been against "pro pers"—legal shorthand for people who represent themselves. Despite published cases and court procedures that dictate that someone who represents himself or herself is held to the same standard as lawyers, in practice that's not the case. Judges will bend over backward to insure not only that the unrepresented litigant gets a fair hearing, but also to insure that it **appears** to the unrepresented litigant that he or she is getting a fair hearing. And "pro pers," unlike many lawyers, simply don't take "No" for an answer. They will read a book, maybe two, and, as proof that "a little knowledge is a dangerous thing," will go into court armed with every supposition or suggestion, no matter in what context it was written, that agrees with their point of view.

If and when they lose, which statistically is quite often, they will appeal and appeal and appeal, file new lawsuits, attempt to invent new theories. A perfect example of how a non-lawyer can clutter up the system is a prisoner whom we'll call Xavier. After being convicted for the second or third time of some felony or other, he set up a "law office" in his cell where he "advertised" that he would do writs, appeals, and every other kind of representation, which would be patently illegal on the outside. Was he going to be tried for the unauthorized practice of law? Hardly, since he was already doing "25 to life." Also, as he prepared all manner of papers for his jailhouse buddies, he never put **his** name on their papers as their legal representative.

A few years after he was incarcerated for his last offense, Xavier petitioned for parole, which was denied. He then filed the first of seven successive civil rights lawsuits against the Board of Corrections in his state. Some of his allegations were so outrageous as to be laughable. He alleged that unnamed members of the board had assaulted and battered him—"kicked, thrashed, beat, socked, truncheoned, humiliated and abused him" (he varied the wording with each lawsuit). He made sure that he filed the cases in federal court, which brought the federal Civil Rights Act—admittedly one of the broadest-defined laws ever written—into play. Time and again, the U.S. District Court dismissed the cases. Each time, the Appeals Courts reinstated the cases using the litmus test for **filing** a lawsuit: "If we accept every fact that the plaintiff pleads as true—regardless of whether or not the plaintiff can prove it—the motion to dismiss cannot be granted."

In Xavier's case, the court finally said, "We are aware that in all probability, Xavier never even met those members of the board whom he alleged beat, kicked, socked and truncheoned him. Nevertheless, no matter how farfetched Xavier's allegations might be, we cannot deny him his right to plead them at this stage of the proceedings."

Nor is Xavier the only one who "practices law without a license." Paralegals have found a legal way to help people. They don't actually **represent** anyone; they simply make sure that papers are prepared correctly so the self-litigant can walk into court with the right documents.

While there are always those who will take advantage of the system, almost to the point of prostituting it (and, on occasion, these may have included some of my "brothers at the bar"), the purpose of this chapter is to give you **reasonable** suggestions of what you might do if your adversary will not consider mediation, if mediation does not work, or if you have decided that you would best be served by entering the legal system.

1) **If there is a legal insurance policy available to you through a reputable company,** look into it. Check it out carefully. What does it include? What does it **not** include? Is there a list of lawyers who will accept insurance payments in full payment of a legal bill? Is the company licensed in your state? Is it financially sound? What is its history?

Lest you think there's no such thing as legal insurance or that it doesn't work, *every* car insurance policy, business insurance policy, professional liability insurance policy, etc. provides that as part of the premium you pay, the insurance company promises to pay for a lawyer on your behalf—and you don't pay a cent extra. And, as we've found above, the insurance companies hire only highly rated law firms to defend you.

2) **Get involved in organizations that provide free (or low cost) legal representation.** Union members have enjoyed low-cost legal services for years. The military has always provided its members with advice (if not actual representation) through the judge advocate general's office, and through referrals to reputable, generally reasonably-priced lawyers. Credit unions sometimes get involved in similar advice or

referral programs. Look around. Such groups are available; you just have to find them.

3) **Write your senator, congressman or local legislator** and press for such things as state controls on what lawyers can charge and a broad-based legal insurance program, even one administered by the state or county. There are such things as Legal Services for Seniors, Legal Aid programs, the Public Defender's Office and outreach programs such as the Rural Legal Assistance Program. Don't be afraid to ask your state, county, local or even federal government what's available to help you.

4) **When you "shop" for a lawyer, after you have determined that he or she has a good reputation, negotiate a firm, fixed fee for your representation, or, failing that, a "high-low" range if the attorney is charging on an hourly basis.** Lawyers don't like to do that, for obvious reasons, but if enough of us insisted on it, the public's will would prevail. If you disagree, ask your doctor what "managed care" has done to what he or she earns. It may not be popular, but it can work—and it might even cut back on the proliferation of lawsuits that plague our society.

5) **When you are seeking a contingency fee lawyer for an injury or the like, negotiate your percentage.** Refuse arrangements that exceed 25 percent up to the time trial starts, 33⅓ percent if it goes through trial. Don't kid yourself: a contingency fee lawyer is no better than any other lawyer, and the fact that he or she is more expensive does **not** mean he or she is "better"—only greedier. And you will certainly find **some** lawyer who will take the case on a 25 to 33⅓ percent basis. Remember, personal injury contingency fee work is the "fat" of the practice.

6) **If the case is relatively simple—and most cases are not complex—consider using a paralegal to help you with the paperwork.** It will cost you about 10 percent of what you'd pay a lawyer for similar work.

7) **Visit the county law library.** Law librarians are well known for their helpful attitude. Most of them are not

lawyers. Lawyers know where to go to find the books they need. They went through law school, where they learned to do legal research in their first year. Generally, their need for law librarians is about the same as their need for street sweepers, unless the arrangement of the books has somehow changed. So, except for you, the need for law librarians is not what it once was. As a result, they will help guide you to the right books, and although they are prohibited by law from giving you legal advice, they know the direction in which to point you to find most, if not all, of what you need.

Incidentally, once you are there, don't be afraid to ask a lawyer who's doing research in the law library to help guide you to a book or series of books that will help answer your problem. I've always been very generous with my free advice when I'm there, and most lawyers I know are really good people at heart when it comes to being helpful in that vein.

Many is the day I've seen a "pro per" hitting the books. Despite everything you might have heard, most law books, particularly case law books, are not written in "legalese" but in pretty plain understandable English. If there is an occasional Latin phrase like *res ipsa loquitur or reductio ad absurdum* (which means reducing a thing to its most absurd example), you simply ask the directions to *Black's Law Dictionary*. If you run into "legalisms" like *equitable estoppel, statute of frauds*, or the like, you go either to *Black's Law Dictionary*, to the index of the particular book or set of books you're using, or to a special book called *Words and Phrases* which will guide you to one or more cases where the court defined it.

Ultimately, you'll be surprised at how easy legal research can be. Like swimming, riding a motor scooter or eating Brussels sprouts, no one ever said it was the easiest thing in the world, but it's certainly not beyond the reasonable ability of anyone with a modicum of intelligence. You will find that as you get into it, it not only becomes easier, but, like Brussels sprouts, may even become an acquired taste.

8) **If you can't have a mediation clause in your contract, at least try to get an arbitration clause in.** Earlier in this book, I said that arbitration was not necessarily the best way to resolve problems. There are many negatives to steer you away from it. But it is still cheaper and simpler by far than litigation, and the cards are never stacked against the "pro per" because *facts, not law,* govern the outcome of the case.

9) **Talk—and keep talking—with your would-be adversary, with your would-be adversary's friend, or with anyone else who can "get him or her to sit down and talk" before both of you decide to go to a lawyer.** If need be, and if you can't mediate, at least try to get someone you both respect and trust to try to help you solve the problem.

10) **Don't be afraid to question the cost while you're getting the monthly bills, not afterward.** One of the biggest mistakes both lawyers and clients make is thinking, "We'll get it all worked out in the end." **Communication is always the key to a successful relationship, whether with a doctor, a wife, a child, or a lawyer.**

11) **Choose your lawyer as you would choose a friend.** A lawyer can be "the best lawyer in town," according to some people. But if that lawyer seems too busy to give you the time you need, or if you feel there's something about the person that might make it difficult for you to get along and work well together, listen to your intuition, hark to the danger signals, and interview the next lawyer.

12) **Don't be afraid to change lawyers in midstream.** Nothing is worse than losing confidence in your lawyer and then feeling helpless to do anything about it. You don't need two enemies and you don't need a two-front war: you vs. your adversary and you vs. your lawyer. A client is **always** free to discharge a lawyer for any reason or for **no** reason. Although lawyers do everything in their power to convince you otherwise, *you* are paying the lawyer, *you* are the boss, and *you* have the **absolute right** to change your lawyer at any time. And at no penalty or extra cost to you. I cannot stress this point too strongly. A lawyer is nothing more than

your hired help—high-priced hired help, talented hired help, but hired help nonetheless.

13) **If you and your lawyer ultimately have a falling out over legal fees, demand arbitration.** It's pretty common in most, if not all, states. Under this system, you, the client, get "two bites at the apple." A lawyer must advise you that you have the right to fee arbitration before he or she can sue you for fees. Even though, in many cases, lawyers sit on the fee arbitration panel, they know that they've been charged with a civic duty and I have always found that they try to be as fair as if they were sitting on a jury. If you don't like the result of the fee arbitration, you still have the right to go to court over the result.

14) **If you must have a lawyer, insist on having a written contract—and make sure you read and understand that contract.** Don't hesitate to make changes, initial them and have your lawyer initial them. These are the ground rules under which you will operate, and, like a baseball game or a bridge game, things always go smoother when both parties understand the rules.

15) **Don't telephone your lawyer unless you absolutely have to!** Being involved with a lawyer makes anyone understandably nervous. Being involved in a lawsuit makes you even more so. The lawyer is the surrogate father or mother—the kindly, all-knowing authority figure who listens to your problems, calms you down, and invariably tells you not to worry, he or she is on top of the situation. Calling your lawyer ten times a day, or even five, or even once a week may be gratifyingly reassuring to you. Just remember, the case is not moving forward one bit faster. And each time you call it's ".2 hour" for the lawyer.

I'm sure that if you use your mind, and hopefully the newly honed creative skills that you have learned from reading this book, you'll come up with even more ideas. And then, besides thinking like a lawyer, you'll be part of the solution. You'll be helping society and yourself to take back the power.

Closing Statement

"The illegal we do immediately.
The unconstitutional takes a little longer."
— **Henry Kissinger**

AWS AND LAWYERS are absolutely, fundamentally, necessary to our way of life. We are proud of saying we are a society of laws, not of men; that no man is above the law; and that the rule of law is above any rule created by man. These are basic truisms with which no one can seriously disagree. Were it otherwise, we would revert back to the time when a particularly strong cave man could seize a smaller man by the scruff of the neck and force him to "evenly" trade a carrot for a cow. And a wife could be stolen with impunity unless the weaker man could surround himself with sufficient allies to defeat his tormentor.

Yet, despite the fact that we are a modern, civilized society, all too often it seems as though the wealthy magnate or company can defeat or outlast the middle-class or poor citizen.

Am I somehow turning cannibal by bashing a profession that has given me a good living for better than half my life? No, I am not. I realize that with all their faults, lawyers are neither better nor worse than anyone else in our society. At best, they perform a needed function honorably and diligently. They are among the most loyal friends and colleagues I've ever known. Most are honest, trustworthy pillars of their communities. A few are bad apples—no more, no less, than in any other profession or occupation.

But I am tired of seeing lawyers constantly vilified, being invariably rated either the lowest or next to the lowest on published scales of personal and professional integrity. I've heard my share of lawyer jokes and laughed at them, knowing that all too often there's more than a shred of truth beneath the bitterness. When I told our graphic designer that I was writing this book, he offered to do the cover for free, "as a public service."

It is time for us to stop running from the accusations and defending against them. It is time for us to *listen* for a change—something we lawyers are all too often loath to do. I would like to see a world where lawyers come back to where they were 150 years ago—wise counselors, known for their understanding and compassion, their balance and wisdom, and, most of all, for their integrity.

No one says the world is fair. My wife, the most exemplary teacher I've ever known, a person who influences our future every day, one young human being at a time, gets paid just under $40,000 a year. Dennis Rodman, Mike Tyson, the Spice Girls and Jerry Seinfeld earn *millions* of dollars—more in a single season than my wife and I will earn together during our lifetimes. There's nothing I can do to change that.

But since I've been on the inside of law for so long, I feel that I *can* change the way people think and act when it comes to resolving their problems. And if I can help change the way people think about law and lawyers, in the way they react when they hear the word "lawyer," if I can somehow open up the door to a better relationship between the profession and its clients—and most important, if I can somehow, without being preachy, bring our profession back into the repute it once had and could have again—then the slings and arrows that may be hurled at me by my colleagues and by anyone else who chooses to do so, will be well worth it.

Questions to Consider Asking Before You Hire an Attorney

HERE ARE SOME QUESTIONS you might consider asking your lawyer. Don't be embarrassed to do so and don't feel ashamed. You are contemplating hiring the lawyer as your professional employee. You have every right to get direct answers to your questions ahead of time. If the lawyer refuses to answer them or answers them other than with honesty and candor, I suggest you consult other lawyers until you get answers with which you feel comfortable.

General
1. How long have you been in practice?
2. How many cases have you actually tried before a jury? Before a court?
3. How many cases similar to mine have you actually tried before a jury? Before a court?
4. What were the results in those cases?
5. How many cases similar to mine have you settled?
6. Were the results in those cases satisfactory to the client(s)?
7. Would you be willing to give me the name and address of the client(s) you represented in that case? I'd like to ask them about their experience.
8. Give me your best estimate of the result you foresee in my case if everything I have told you is substantially true.
9. Do you believe in alternative dispute resolution—mediation or arbitration?

10. On how many occasions have you participated in alternative dispute resolution?
11. What were the results in those cases?
12. Might I see your standard written retainer agreement? Do you mind if I take it home and look it over for a couple of days before I sign it and return it to you?
13. What is your hourly charge?
14. Do you charge for: (a) long distance phone calls; (b) photo-copies; (c) your secretary's time? (d) faxes? (e) what other cost charges?
15. Do you charge interest on bills more than 30 days old? At what rate?
16. Do you have a device on your telephone that tells you exactly how much time elapses on each call?
17. Do you bill by $1/10$ hour increments? Do you have a minimum incremental charge?
18. Would you be willing to accept my case on a firm, fixed-fee basis? How much would that cost?
19. Are you willing to give me a written estimate, top to bottom, of how much you believe it would cost me to have you repre-sent me from the beginning to the end of my case, including out-of-pocket costs?
20. Would you be willing to give me a "cap"—a not-to-exceed figure—on my legal bills if you represent me?
21. Will I be able to recover all or any of my attorneys' fees or costs from the other side?
22. What is your best estimate on how long it will take to get my case to court?
23. Would you be willing to take my case on a contingency fee basis? At what percentage?
24. Have you ever been the subject of a State Bar disciplinary investigation? What was the result?
25. Have you ever sued a client for fees? What was the result?
26. Do I have the right to change lawyers at any time if I am dis-satisfied with your services? (If the lawyer answers anything but an unqualified "Yes," get out of that office as soon as pos-sible.)

27. Do I have the right to be informed in a timely manner about every aspect of my case?
28. Are you willing to send me copies of all letters you send and receive on my behalf at no extra charge?
29. Does your firm normally engage in "team billing"—will more than one lawyer be working on my case at a time?
30. If a lawyer other than you will be handling any aspect of my case, will I have a chance to meet and approve of that lawyer before he or she does any work for me?
31. Will I be billed for the time you spend supervising or checking the work of a junior associate?
32. Can I expect to receive a detailed, written bill each month?
33. Do I have the right to question any bill I receive?
34. If we have a disagreement, do I have the right to fee arbitration? (If the lawyer tells you "No," that's inaccurate. See another lawyer immediately.)
35. What can I do to reduce your fees and the costs of the case?

Personal Injury
(Ask these questions in addition to those above)

1. What percentage would you charge me to represent my interests?
2. I am willing to pay 25 percent of the **net** recovery. Are you willing to accept that? (Many lawyers will. Do not be afraid or ashamed to negotiate the percentage the lawyer receives. In no event should it exceed 33⅓ percent of the gross recovery.)
3. I have my own medical insurance. Do you charge anything to deal with my carrier after you settle the case?
4. Is your fee based on a percentage of the **gross** or a percentage *after* my costs and bills are paid? (Although it is common practice to charge on the gross, it is much fairer to take a percentage of the **net**—after all, *you're* paying those costs).
5. What has your experience been with _____ (the other party's insurance carrier)?
6. How many cases similar to mine have you settled?
7. What results have you achieved in each instance?

8. Give me an estimate of what you think my case is worth— or how you would arrive at an estimate of what the case is worth?

9. Give me an estimate of how long you think it will take for my case to be concluded if it has to go all the way through trial.

10. How much do you estimate I will spend on expert witnesses? Depositions? Filing fees?

Divorce
(Ask these questions in addition to the general questions)

1. Do you regularly use the services of a mediator to cut down on costs?

3. Can you recommend a mediator to talk with me and my spouse before we spend a lot of money on lawyers?

3. Do you have a dissomaster or other computer-assisted device to let me know the range of child support and/or alimony I will likely have to pay or will receive? Do you charge extra to give me a printout?

4. What is your philosophy on trying to settle divorce cases?

5. How soon can I get into court to obtain (a) alimony; (b) child support; (c) a restraining order?

6. How can I make sure I pay as little attorneys' fees as possible?

Probate
(Ask these questions in addition to general questions)

1. Do you charge separate fees for being executor or administrator **and** for serving as the attorney for the estate?

2. What is the statutory fee for an estate of this size?

3. In what percentage of the probates you have handled have you sought extraordinary attorneys' fees?

4. Do you foresee anything in this probate that would lead you to believe you would seek extraordinary fees? What things would those be?

5. What do you believe will be the total fees and costs expended on this case?

6. How long will it take to probate and close this estate?

7. How long will it take before the assets in this case are distributed?
8. How much do you think taxes will be on this estate?
9. What can you do to reduce the taxes and the time it will take to probate this estate?

Sample Attorney's
Written Retainer Agreement

THIS IS AN ACTUAL COPY of the retainer fee agreement I am presently using in my practice. I hope it is clear, non-frightening, and informative.

1. SCOPE OF OUR RELATIONSHIP WITH ONE ANOTHER:
You are hiring us as your attorneys to represent you in the following matter: *(Description of subject matter of the representation)*

ATTORNEYS' DUTIES: This is our commitment to you: **Our Best Effort.** We promise to give you all of our experience, training and energies in our representation of you. **Prompt Return of Phone Calls.** If we cannot return a call within a day (which should rarely happen) we will have a staff member call to explain why the call has not been returned and when it will be returned. If you consider your call urgent, please say so and other less urgent matters or meetings will be put aside or delayed so that we can take care of your matter. **The Truth.** We promise to tell you the truth as we see it. **Kept Promises.** If we tell you we will perform a service, we will do so when promised. If there is a reason work on your matter is delayed, we will tell you what is happening and when the work is performed. **To Keep You Informed.** You will be promptly informed of all developments in your case. **Decisions.** Some decisions are made by the attorney, others are made by the client. You will be made aware of any significant decision that we intend to make and will have a full opportunity to participate in the process. You will be given all relevant information relating to any decision that you are to make with sufficient advance time for you to consider the possible courses. If there is any question as to whether you or we are to make the decision, you will have the decision making authority unless you decide to delegate it to us. **Detailed Billing.** You have the right to know in detail what you are being charged for. Our bills are quite specific regarding both fees and costs. We will promptly answer any question that you have about our bills. **To Be Punctual.** If we have an appointment with you, we will be on time. If we are delayed we will make an effort to reach you to lessen your inconvenience.

We will provide those legal services reasonably required to represent you in this matter. If a court action is filed, we will represent you through trial and post-trial motions. This agreement does not cover our representation of your interests on appeal. Unless you and we make a different agreement in writing, this agreement will govern all future services we perform for you.

You authorize us to take or defend actions against any and all persons or other entities who, in our sole discretion, should be joined in order to best protect your interest with respect to matters covered by this agreement.

Many of the things we do for you are done outside of your presence, so you should understand that we will note the time spent not only in meetings with you or appearances at court, but also for time used in telephone calls, legal research, travel time, trial preparation, letter writing, drafting agreements or other papers or meetings with other attorneys, the court or witnesses. Please be assured that we will take whatever time is necessary, but we will not spend unnecessary time on your case. In that regard, your courtesy and cooperation with us and with our staff would be appreciated, and anything you can do to save our time will reduce your costs.

It is impossible to predict with any real accuracy how much of our time will be expended on your matter, since so much depends upon factors over which we have no control, e.g., court calendars, the complexity of issues and the extent to which the adverse parties and their attorneys will or will not cooperate with each other and our office.

CLIENT'S DUTIES: This is your commitment to us: You agree to be truthful with us, to cooperate with us, to keep us informed of developments that may affect our representation of your interests, to respond promptly to any requests we make of you to assist us or that may become necessary for us to protect your best interests, to pay our bills on time, and to keep us advised of your address, telephone number and whereabouts at all times.

2. MINIMUM FEE / DEPOSIT/ LEGAL FEES AND BILLING PRACTICES

We both agree that it is crucial that we, as attorneys, be in a position to represent your interests without the added concern of whether or not and when we are going to be paid. Disagreements over fees strain a relationship and we cannot be placed in a position where we have a dispute with you at the same time we are representing your interests.

a) **Initial retainer and cost deposit.** You agree to pay us an initial retainer of $_____ as follows: $_____ on signing this agreement and an additional $_____ within ___ days thereafter. Although this retainer is nonrefundable, our hourly charges will be credited against this fee, with respect to this matter only. It will not be credited against fees for other work that you may ask us to do for you.

In addition to the retainer fee, you agree to pay us an initial cost deposit of $_____ within ten days of signing this agreement. This deposit will be applied solely for out-of pocket costs incurred in representing your interests (See paragraph (f) below, for a description of these costs). The cost deposit will be held in a segregated trust account for your benefit, and any sums not used by the end of our representation of your interests will be returned to you.

b) **Standard fee rate.** You agree to pay for our services at the rate of $_____ per hour. We will give you at least sixty (60) days' written notice if we intend to raise our hourly fee. Unless you advise us otherwise in writing prior to the expiration of the notice, you agree to pay us the stated adjustment in hourly rates after the expiration of the 60-day notice period.

c) **Telephone time and other charges.** We charge you for time we spend on telephone calls relating to your matter, including calls to or from you, opposing counsel, witnesses, investigators, court personnel, or any other persons. Although we generally do not "double team," there may be instances where legal personnel assigned to your matter may, of necessity, confer among themselves or work together on your matter. When they do confer, each person will charge for the time expended. Likewise, if more than one of our legal personnel attends a meeting, court hearing, arbitration, or other proceeding, each will charge for the time spent. We will charge for waiting time in court and elsewhere, and for travel time, both local and out of town. However, intercity air travel time is ordinarily not charged at full rate. We charge for our time in minimum units of .1 (¹⁄₁₀th) of an hour.

d) **Billing practices: timely payment expected. Each month, we will send you a detailed statement for legal fees and costs incurred. We expect that you will pay that statement in full within ten (10) days. This is important for both of us: it will enable you to control billing and costs without what you might feel to be an unreasonable buildup; and it will enable us to keep our own accounts current and avoid a backlog of accounts receivable which forces us to take time away from the practice of law. If you have not paid your bill by the tenth day, you may expect a call from us on the eleventh day to find out why you have not paid. If you have not paid your bill in full, within thirty (30) days of billing, we will give you written notice that unless you have paid the bill within ten (10) additional days, or if other mutually acceptable arrangements are not made to pay or secure the account, you agree that we have good cause to terminate this agreement and render no further legal services for you. IF THERE IS ANY TIME THAT YOUR CURRENT BILL EXCEEDS $1,000 AND YOU HAVE NOT PAID US WITHIN TEN (10) DAYS OF BILLING, YOU AGREE THAT WE HAVE GOOD CAUSE TO TERMINATE THIS AGREEMENT. INTEREST; TRUTH-IN-LENDING DISCLOSURE: ANY SUMS NOT PAID WITHIN THIRTY (30) DAYS OF BILLING WILL BEAR INTEREST AT THE RATE OF 10 PERCENT PER ANNUM.**

e) **Costs.** We will incur various out-of-pocket costs and expenses in performing legal services under this agreement. You agree to pay for those costs and expenses in addition to the hourly fees. These costs and expenses commonly include filing fees fixed by law or assessed by courts and/or other agencies, mediator's or arbitrator's fees, process server's fees, court reporter's fees, expert witness fees, long distance telephone calls, fax costs, messenger and other delivery fees, postage, parking and other local travel expenses, photocopying and other reproduction costs, charges for computer research time, clerical staff overtime, and other similar items. All costs and expenses will be charged at our cost. Payment for costs is your responsibility.

f) **Out-of-Town Travel.** You agree to pay transportation, meals, lodging, car rental and gasoline, out-of-town per diem at $50.00 per day, and all other costs of necessary out-of-town travel by our personnel. You will also be charged the standard hourly rates for the time legal personnel spend traveling once they have arrived in the general out-of-town area where services are to take place. Intercity air travel time will not normally be charged at the full rate, but we will charge you a reasonable rate for such time.

g) **Experts.** To aid in the preparation and presentation of your case, it may become necessary to hire expert witnesses, consultants, or investigators. We will not hire such persons unless you agree to pay their fees and charges. We will select any expert witnesses, consultants, or investigators to be hired. We may also retain consultant expert attorneys on your behalf to assist in the trial or preparation of your case. **Such experts may, in our opinion, be so critical to the proper and effective preparation and presentation of your case that we will ordinarily not proceed to trial without such experts. If you and we cannot agree on the necessity of any experts and their compensation, you agree that we may terminate this contract and our services to you by giving fifteen (15) days' written notice.**

h) **Cost deposit and continuing obligation to pay costs.**

THIS OFFICE DOES NOT NORMALLY ADVANCE COSTS ON BEHALF OF A CLIENT. WE ARE A LAW FIRM, NOT A FINANCIAL INSTITUTION. THAT IS WHY IT IS ABSOLUTELY NECESSARY THAT YOU MAINTAIN A COST DEPOSIT ACCOUNT WITH US AT ALL TIMES.

As indicated above, you will make an initial cost deposit with us. Whenever your deposit is exhausted and the amount in our trust account is less than reasonably required to proceed with reasonable prosecution or defense of your interests, you will be required to make a further deposit to the extent necessary to replenish the minimum trust account requirement, and this amount must be paid within ten days of our notifying you of this requirement. Once a trial or arbitration has been set, we will require you to pay all sums then owed to us and to deposit the attorney's fees, costs (including expert's fees) we estimate will be incurred in preparation for and completing the trial or arbitration, as well as estimated jury fees, reporter's fees and/or arbitration fees likely to be assessed. Those sums may exceed the minimum trust account requirement and we make no promise to you that these will be the total fees and costs you are obligated to pay. **If you have not paid all reasonable costs within fifteen (15) days of our advising you that we need to have them paid, you agree that we may terminate this contract and our services to you by giving fifteen (15) days' written notice.**

ESTIMATE OF TOTAL FEES: In any case where the fee is expected to exceed one thousand dollars ($1,000), California law requires us to give our best estimate of the total costs and fees you might be expected to pay in this matter. Please understand that this is an **ESTIMATE ONLY** and may not be the maximum. With respect to the matter for which you are retaining us, we believe that the maximum cost to you shall not exceed $_____ .

3. COMMITMENT TO ALTERNATIVE DISPUTE RESOLUTION:

This office subscribes to a policy of attempting to resolve disputes through alternative dispute resolution in forums other than court if at all possible. These forums include mediation, negotiation, and, if these procedures do not work, either binding or advisory arbitration. You acknowledge that we have explained these procedures to you in

advance of your signing this agreement. The reason we adopt this policy is that we have found that court proceedings are expensive, time consuming, and frequently do not resolve the differences in a manner satisfactory to the client. We have found it to be cheaper, faster, and more conducive to overall peaceful resolution of disputes to use alternative dispute resolution. By signing this engagement contract, you agree to participate in good faith in alternative dispute resolution procedures.

4. LIEN. You hereby grant us a lien on any and all causes of action that are the subject of our representation under this agreement. Our lien will be for any sums owing to us at the conclusion of our services. The lien will attach to any recovery you may obtain, whether by arbitration award, judgment, settlement or otherwise, and will apply to any legal work we have done for you.

5. DISCHARGE AND WITHDRAWAL. You may discharge us at any time, with or without cause. We may withdraw with your consent or for good cause. Good cause includes your breach of this agreement, your refusal to cooperate with us or to follow or advice on a material matter, your refusal to pay our billings in a timely manner, your refusal to provide materials for your case that we request of you, our discovery that you have not been forthright and truthful with us, or any fact or circumstance that would render our continuing representation of you unlawful or unethical. If we choose to withdraw, we must give you no less than fifteen (15) days' notice, unless such withdrawal is a matter of urgency.

When our services conclude, all unpaid charges will become immediately due and payable. After our services conclude we will, upon your written request, deliver your file to you along with any funds or property of yours in our possession, save and except any funds to which our lien has attached, provided that you agree to pay us all costs incurred in making duplicate copies of those documents that we deem necessary for the maintenance of a reasonable backfile in your matter.

6. NO WARRANTY OR GUARANTY. We make no warranty or guaranty, either express or implied, of a successful termination of this matter, nor can we make any promise that you will be satisfied with the result. Any expression made to you, such as the value of your case or the chances of winning or losing, are expressions of opinion only, made with reference to those facts we know at that time; and such opinion is not in any way a promise to you.

7. **DISPUTES.** If we have a dispute over fees or anything else, either one of us has the absolute right to have the claim submitted to binding arbitration on demand. If we must sue you or arbitrate a claim for fees against you and we win, the arbitrator or court shall award us, in addition to our recovery, all attorneys' fees and costs that we incur in bringing the matter to the court or arbitrator.

8. **NOTICES.** All notices, including notices that might normally require personal service between us, shall be deemed effective if mailed to you at your last known address, provided that we mail it to you first-class mail, postage prepaid. The service shall be deemed complete ten days after we mail it to you. You agree to waive personal service of such notices.

9. **LIMITED POWER OF ATTORNEY TO ENDORSE CHECKS OR DRAFTS.** You expressly authorize us to endorse your name on any checks, drafts, or proceeds received in your name or for your benefit, to deposit these sums in our trust account, and to make distribution to you at your last known address after first deducting any sums from such monies as shall then be due to us.

10. **STATEMENT OF ERRORS AND OMISSIONS (MALPRACTICE) INSURANCE:**

Although it is not required that we be covered by errors and omissions (malpractice) insurance, California Law requires that we advise you whether or not we are covered by such insurance and, if so, the name of the carrier. This office is insured by _____ Insurance Company for Errors and Omissions up to a limit of $_____.

11. **DESTRUCTION OF FILES.** It is our policy to destroy all files five (5) years after we have concluded our representation of your interests. It is your obligation to advise us at the conclusion of our representation whether you would like your file returned to you at that time. You agree to provide us with your most recent current address up to five (5) years after we cease to represent you. Ten (10) days before we destroy your file, we will give you written notice that we intend to destroy it. If you do not pick up the file within that time, we will destroy the file and we will be under no further obligation to you.

12. **WAIVER OF CONFLICT.** In certain situations, we may represent more than one client (for example, a husband and wife, or two or more business partners or associates). It is possible that at some time during or after our representation of your interests, there could arise a conflict of interest between the two of you. **You hereby agree that each of you, by signing this agreement, specifically waives any conflict that might arise out of our representing your interests at the inception of this agreement.**

13. **NO ATTORNEY-CLIENT RELATIONSHIP ESTABLISHED BY MERELY DISCUSSING YOUR MATTER WITH YOU.** You agree that the fact that we may have spoken with one another by telephone or in person does not establish an attorney-client relationship between us. **We will take no action on your behalf, nor are you authorized to act on any opinion we may have expressed to you, unless and until you have signed and returned at least one copy of this agreement to us.**

NOTICE TO CLIENT: WE ARE NOT YOUR ATTORNEYS, WE DO NOT REPRESENT YOU, AND THERE IS NO ATTORNEY-CLIENT RELATIONSHIP BETWEEN US UNTIL SUCH TIME AS YOU HAVE SIGNED AND RETURNED THIS CONTRACT TO US. THIS IS A CONTRACT—A LEGAL AND BINDING DOCUMENT. READ IT AND MAKE SURE YOU UNDERSTAND IT. BY SIGNING THIS DOCUMENT, YOU ACKNOWLEDGE THAT YOU UNDERSTAND AND AGREE TO ALL TERMS AND THAT YOU WILL BE RESPONSIBLE FOR ALL OBLIGATIONS INCURRED. IF THERE IS MORE THAN ONE SIGNATOR, EACH OF YOU IS FULLY LIABLE FOR THE PERFORMANCE

OF ALL SIGNATORS. IF YOU ARE SIGNING ON BEHALF OF A CORPORATION, YOU AGREE THAT YOU ARE PERSONALLY LIABLE AS WELL.

Dated: _____

LAW OFFICES OF HUGO N. GERSTL

by: _____   _____
    HUGO N. GERSTL   CLIENT:

Index

Acknowledgments

SPECIAL THANKS to each of these people who have contributed their knowledge, inspiration and friendship to this, as to other ventures in my life:

The Honorable Nat A. Agliano of Salinas, California
Dennis Alexander of Seaside, California
Jennifer Allen of Mansfield, Texas
The Honorable John N. Anton of Pebble Beach, California
Shane K. Brock of Carmel, California
Ron & Terri Chaplan of Carmel, California
Herb & Sharon Chelner of Chatsworth, California
Charles Chrietzberg of Monterey, California
Tres Codey & Haruna Isa of Alexandria, Virginia
Tracy & Jake Corchine of Cameron Park, California
The Honorable William D. Curtis of Monterey,. California
William B. Daniels, Esq. of Monterey, California
Kathleen DeVanna Fish and Robert Fish of Monterey, California
Susan Kay Fisher of Pacific Grove, California
The Late Alfred Gerstl & Trudy Gerstl, my beloved parents
Alfred & Ursula Gerstl of Vienna, Austria
Carrie Gerstl of San Diego, California
Jeff & Rachel Gerstl of San Diego, California
Joshua & Rachel Gerstl of Haifa, Israel
Lorraine Gerstl of Carmel, California
Ted, Candy & Jesse Gerstl of Pieve a Elici, Tuscany, Italy
Harmon, Margie, Tammi & Jason Glantz of Chino Hills, California
Janet Gluckman & Robert Fleck of Las Vegas, Nevada

Richard D. Gorman, Esq. & Claire L. Gorman of
  Carmel Highlands, California
Rabbi & Mrs. Bruce Greenbaum of Carmel, California
Nadine Guarrera of Monterey, California
River & Diana Case Gurtin of Pebble Beach. California
Laurie Harper of San Francisco, California
Teresa Hartnett & Paul Matulac of Alexandria, Virginia
The Honorable George E. Honts III of Lexington, Virginia
Alan Irwin of Seaside, California
Ramy Jarallah of Newport Beach, California
The Late Gary Jennings
Alan Kaplan, Esq. of Carmel, California
Paul Karrer of Monterey, California
Harry, Margie, Bryan, Michael, Aviva & Leah Klompas
Joyce Krieg of Monterey, California
Mel Kryger of Salinas, California
Susan D. Kucher of Monterey, California
Donald & Barbara Newman Lessne of Hollywood, Florida
The Honorable Robert Lieblich and Sharon Lieblich, Esq. of
  Alexandria, Virginia
Lynne McAdoo of Kansas City, Missouri
The Late John I. Mehrholz
Kathy Mehrholz of Springdale, Arkansas
Greg, Karen & Roslyn Migdale of Carmel, California
Ron Montana of San Jose, California
Michaeleen Moraz, Esq. of Monterey, California
Zvi Morik of Tel Aviv, Israel
Howard & Michele Morton of Carmel Valley, California
Jean C. & Birgit Mouton of Carmel, California
Alan & Beverley Movson of Carmel, California
Timothy Neal of Pacific Grove, California
Mickey Nowicki of Monterey, California
The Honorable Robert O'Farrell of Carmel Valley, California
Colleen M. & Alvin Olis of Monterey, California
Kristi Padley of Portland, Maine
The Honorable Harkjoon Paik of Carmel Valley, California
Troy Scott Parker of Boulder, Colorado

Norman & Cathy Pieters of North Miami, Florida
Beth Piña of Carmel Valley, California
John Pisto of Monterey, California
Clark Savage of Carmel, California
Steven & Lori Schulman of Boca Raton, Florida and
    Pebble Beach, California
Calvin Seldin, Esq. & Lila Seldin of Pacific Grove, California
Joyce Servis of Caldwell, New Jersey
Dr. Sanford M. Shapero & Linda Eng of Beverly Hills, California
The Honorable Richard M. Silver of Carmel Highlands, California
Major General & Mrs. Nolan Sklute of Las Vegas, Nevada
Brad & Susan Smith of Salinas, California
The Honorable James Stewart of San Jose, California
Maestro Clark E. Suttle of Salinas, California
Mary Jane Thomas of Prunedale, California
Marilyn Tully of Carmel, California
Charles & Fredia Watnick of Woodland Hills, California
Linda Webster of Kansas City, Missouri
Eugene & Ina Winick of New York, New York

About the Author

HUGO GERSTL takes on the legal profession from a unique prospective: he's been a practicing trial lawyer for more than thirty-three years. Along the way, he's taken on the Government and large companies and tried cases in seventeen states and the District of Columbia, Along with his share of battle scars, he's also achieved a $1.8 million jury verdict and a $1.2 million settlement, giving him entree into the Million Dollar Advocates Forum.

He has served as an arbitrator for the Monterey County, California Superior Court for over twenty years and has served as Judge Pro Temp. in that county's court system.

He and his wife have raised five now grown children, only one of whom has been involved in the legal profession. He claims he is still waiting for her to come to her senses.